Entrepreneurial Enlightenment

Entrepreneurial Enlightenment
Secrets to Building a Spiritually-Aligned Business

Alex Wealthfield

Mindful Pages

Published in 2024

ISBN: 9789358815368 (PB)
ISBN: 9789358815085 (eBook)

Published by

Mindful Pages
Imprint of Alpha Editions LLC
312 W. 2nd St #1834
Casper, WY 82601, USA
www.mindfulpagespublishers.com

Contents

Setting the Stage

Welcome to a journey like no other - a journey that intertwines the ambitious energy of entrepreneurship with the profound depth of spiritual wisdom. "Entrepreneurial Enlightenment: Secrets to Building a Spiritually-Aligned Business" is more than just a guide; it's an invitation to redefine what success means in the business world.

In today's fast-paced, competitive environment, the landscape of entrepreneurship often seems dominated by targets, metrics, and bottom lines. Yet, beneath this surface of numbers and strategies lies a deeper, more meaningful layer – the realm of spirituality. It's where passion, purpose, and inner peace reside, waiting to be integrated into your business journey. This book is your guide to doing just that.

The concept of spirituality in business might seem unconventional at first. After all, aren't spirituality and business on opposite ends of the spectrum? Here's a revelation: they are not just compatible; they are, in fact, deeply interconnected. Spirituality in business is about aligning your work with your inner values, beliefs, and purpose. It's about leading with integrity, building meaningful relationships, and positively impacting the world.

As we dive into this fascinating fusion, let's begin by debunking a common myth: spirituality is not about religion. It's not confined to any particular belief system or practice. Instead, spirituality is about connecting with something greater than ourselves –a sense of purpose, universal values, or the interconnectedness of all things. It's about the inner journey that guides and influences our outer actions.

Why Spiritual Alignment Matters in Business

In entrepreneurship, success is often measured in profit margins and market shares. However, true and lasting success – the kind that is fulfilling on all levels – requires more than just financial gain. It needs spiritual alignment.

A spiritually-aligned business not only thrives financially but also contributes positively to the well-being of its stakeholders, respects the environment, and operates on principles of fairness and compassion. It's a business that understands the importance of nourishing the soul of its leadership, employees, and customers.

But how exactly does spirituality benefit business? For starters, it fosters a more profound sense of purpose and motivation. When your work resonates with your core values, it becomes more than just a job –a mission. This sense of purpose drives innovation, inspires loyalty, and attracts like-minded customers and employees.

Moreover, spiritually-aligned businesses often cultivate a culture of mindfulness, empathy, and resilience. Such an environment improves employee satisfaction and productivity and enhances decision-making and problem-solving abilities. These qualities are invaluable in a world where businesses are increasingly held accountable for their social and environmental impact.

As we embark on this journey together, each section of this book is carefully crafted to guide you through the different facets of integrating spirituality into your entrepreneurial venture.

We begin by exploring the first section, the **Foundations of Spiritual Entrepreneurship**. This part delves into understanding your inner motivations, aligning your business with your spiritual beliefs, and creating a mindful business plan. Here, you'll learn to lay the groundwork for a company that succeeds in the market and resonates with your soul.

In the second section, we venture into **Cultivating Spiritual Leadership**. Leadership is not just about managing teams and making decisions; it's about inspiring, guiding, and setting an example. This section will show you how to lead with consciousness, build a soulful team, and foster an environment of mindful communication.

In the third section, **Strategies for Spiritual and Business Growth**, we'll explore innovative thinking through a spiritual lens, ethical entrepreneurship, and sustainable practices. This part is about growing your business consistent with your spiritual values and contributing positively to society.

Next, we explore the **Expanding Impact and Influence** will take you through purposeful networking, marketing with heart, and giving back to the community. Here, you'll learn how to extend your spiritual influence beyond your business's confines, creating positive change in the wider world.

Finally, in **Personal Growth and Business Evolution**, we address the balance between personal spiritual practices and business activities. This section is devoted to helping you grow alongside your business, adapt to change, and envision the long-term spiritual impact of your entrepreneurial journey.

Each chapter is peppered with real-life stories, practical exercises, and thought-provoking insights to make your reading experience informative but also enjoyable and engaging. Whether you're an aspiring entrepreneur or a seasoned business leader, this book offers a fresh perspective on success that combines the drive for profit with the pursuit of purpose.

"Entrepreneurial Enlightenment: Secrets to Building a Spiritually-Aligned Business" is more than a book; it's a manifesto for a new kind of entrepreneurship. It's an invitation to embark on a transformative journey that will change how you do business and view success and fulfilment.

So, let's turn the page and begin this exciting journey together. Welcome to the world of entrepreneurial enlightenment, where business meets spirituality, and success encompasses wealth and well-being.

As we conclude this introduction, remember that this journey is yours to take at your own pace, in your style. The pages ahead are filled with wisdom, insights, and practical advice, all waiting to help you build a business that's both successful in the traditional sense and spiritually fulfilling and aligned with your deepest values.

Happy reading, and here's to your journey towards entrepreneurial enlightenment!

Part I: Foundations of Spiritual Entrepreneurship

Ch 1. The Entrepreneur's Inner Journey Understanding Your Spiritual Motivations

As we step into entrepreneurship, we often find ourselves driven by various forces: the desire for success, the thrill of innovation, and the dream of making an impact. However, nestled within these ambitions lies a deeper, more profound motivator - our spiritual essence. This chapter guides you to uncovering and embracing this vital aspect of your entrepreneurial spirit.

First, we delve into what it means to have spiritual motivation in business. This is not about financial gain or market dominance but how your deepest beliefs and values can shape and drive your business. It's about understanding how your work reflects your inner self and how this alignment can lead to business success, personal fulfilment, and a greater purpose. Here, we'll explore how to identify and articulate these spiritual motivations and integrate them into the very fabric of your business.

Next, we navigate the vital process of self-reflection and discovery. This journey is personal and profound. It involves peeling back the layers of your ambitions to reveal the core beliefs and values that drive you. We'll guide you in exploring your inner landscape through various exercises and introspective techniques - the passions, experiences, and convictions that define you. This self-awareness is the cornerstone of building a business that is not just successful but also spiritually congruent and fulfilling.

Finally, we address the challenges of staying true to your spiritual motivations in the dynamic and often demanding business world. How do you maintain your spiritual integrity amidst market pressures and financial constraints? How do you make decisions that are both commercially sound and spiritually aligned? We'll explore strategies for navigating these challenges, ensuring your business journey remains anchored to your spiritual truths.

As we embark on this chapter, remember that this is more than just a learning experience; it's an invitation to transform how you view and conduct your business. It's about aligning your entrepreneurial journey with your most profound spiritual motivations, leading to a path of both external success and internal fulfilment. Let's begin this journey with open hearts and minds, ready to discover the true essence of being a spiritually motivated entrepreneur.

Defining Spiritual Motivation in Business

In the dynamic world of entrepreneurship, motivation is often synonymous with profit, growth, and market dominance. However, within the multifaceted layers of business aspirations lies a less explored but equally significant motivator – spiritual motivation. This article delves into the essence of spiritual motivation in entrepreneurship, differentiating it from traditional business drivers and underscoring its role in forging a fulfilling and sustainable business journey.

Spiritual motivation in business transcends the conventional metrics of success. It's not quantifiable by revenue, profit margins, or market share. Instead, it's about finding more profound meaning and purpose in entrepreneurial endeavours. The driving force originates from an entrepreneur's core beliefs, values, and purpose. This motivation is intrinsic, emanating from personal conviction and spiritual understanding.

Unlike traditional business motivations, which are often externally driven and reactive to market trends and financial goals, spiritual motivation is introspective and proactive. It is about aligning business actions with personal spiritual values, leading to a sense of fulfilment that goes beyond financial success.

Conventional business drivers like profit maximization and market competition are essential for the survival and growth of any business. They are tangible, measurable, and crucial for making strategic decisions. However, they do not necessarily cater to the more profound human need for purpose and connection. Spiritual motivation fills this gap by integrating personal values and beliefs into the business equation.

For example, a profit-driven entrepreneur might focus solely on strategies that maximize financial returns, sometimes at the expense of other factors like employee well-being, environmental impact, or ethical considerations. On the other hand, an entrepreneur driven by spiritual motivation will weigh their decisions against a broader spectrum of values, such as community impact, sustainability, and ethical practices. This doesn't mean compromising profitability but seeking a balance where business success and personal values coexist harmoniously.

Aligning Business Goals with Personal Spiritual Beliefs and Values

Aligning business goals with personal spiritual beliefs and values is a transformative process. It starts with self-awareness, understanding one's core values, and what truly matters beyond material success. This could stem from religious beliefs, personal philosophies, a commitment to social and environmental causes, or a desire for personal growth and enlightenment.

The entrepreneurial journey becomes more meaningful when business goals align with these personal spiritual values. Decisions are made based on financial outcomes and how they resonate with the entrepreneur's beliefs. This could manifest in various aspects of the business, such as ethical sourcing of materials, ensuring fair labour practices, adopting eco-friendly operations, or engaging in community development.

Integrating spiritual motivation into business practices does not detract from success; it often enhances it. Customers and clients are increasingly drawn to businesses that stand for something more than just profit. A company that reflects honesty, integrity, and a commitment to broader societal and environmental issues can build a more substantial, more loyal customer base.

Furthermore, spiritually motivated businesses often foster a more positive and productive workplace. When employees see that their work contributes to a greater good and aligns with their values, it increases job satisfaction, loyalty, and motivation. This, in turn, can lead to improved performance, innovation, and a strong company culture.

Challenges and Considerations in Embracing Spiritual Motivation

Embracing spiritual motivation in business is not without its challenges. It requires a delicate balance between staying true to one's values and navigating the practical realities of the business world. There may be times when financial pressures or market demands conflict with spiritual motivations.

One key challenge is the risk of alienating specific stakeholders or customers who may not share the same values or beliefs. It requires a strategic approach to communicate the business's core values inclusively.

Moreover, aligning business practices with spiritual beliefs often requires a long-term perspective. Immediate financial gains may sometimes need to be sacrificed for long-term value-driven goals. This requires patience, resilience, and a deep commitment to one's spiritual convictions.

Many successful entrepreneurs and businesses have embraced spiritual motivation as a core component of their business model. For instance, a tech company might commit to ethical data practices and user privacy, reflecting a more profound value of respect and integrity. A fashion brand might adopt sustainable and ethical production methods that align with environmental stewardship and social responsibility values.

These examples illustrate that spiritual motivation in business is not just a theoretical concept but a practical and impactful approach. By integrating personal values into business practices, entrepreneurs can create enterprises that thrive economically, contribute positively to society, and fulfil more profound spiritual objectives.

Fostering spiritual motivation in an entrepreneurial context begins with introspection. It involves identifying your core values and beliefs and understanding how they can be reflected in your business practices. This might include revisiting your business mission, vision, and strategies to ensure they align with your spiritual motivations.

Engaging with like-minded communities, mentors, or groups can also provide support and inspiration. Networking with other spiritually motivated entrepreneurs can offer insights, shared experiences, and a sense of community.

Additionally, regular reflection and assessment are crucial. This involves periodically evaluating whether your business practices and decisions align with your spiritual values and making necessary adjustments.

The Journey Ahead

As we explore the intersection of spirituality and entrepreneurship, it's clear that spiritual motivation is a powerful and transformative force in business. It goes beyond mere financial success, touching upon deeper aspects of meaning, purpose, and impact.

By embracing spiritual motivation, entrepreneurs can embark on a journey that leads to business success, personal fulfilment, and a positive contribution to the world. This journey is not always easy but undoubtedly rewarding, offering a path to a more holistic and meaningful approach to entrepreneurship.

In the ever-evolving landscape of business, where challenges and opportunities abound, embracing spiritual motivation offers a path to succeed and thrive with purpose and integrity. It's a journey of aligning one's deepest values with their entrepreneurial aspirations, creating businesses that prosper, elevate, and inspire.

Self-Reflection and Discovery

In entrepreneurship, understanding the 'why' behind your business endeavours is as crucial as the 'how' of achieving success. This 'why' is often rooted in our deeper spiritual motivations, an aspect that gets overshadowed by the more tangible aspects of business. Self-reflection and discovery is critical to uncovering these motivations, offering a compass for navigating the entrepreneurial journey with purpose and authenticity.

The entrepreneurship journey is often external – driven by market trends, customer needs, and competitive strategies. However, the internal journey –self-reflection and discovery – is equally critical. This internal journey is about understanding who you are, what drives you, and what you believe in. It's about aligning your business with your deeper spiritual motivations, ensuring that your entrepreneurial pursuits are successful and fulfilling.

Self-reflection in entrepreneurship involves asking introspective questions: What are my core values? What is my vision for my life, and how does my business fit into this? What impact do I want to have through my company? The answers to these questions lay the groundwork for a business that is an extension of your inner self, a vehicle for expressing your deepest values and beliefs.

Exercises for Uncovering Spiritual Motivations

> **Vision Mapping:** Create a visual representation of your ideal life and business. Use images, words, and symbols to depict your values, goals, and what you find spiritually fulfilling. This exercise helps in visualizing how your business aligns with your vision.

> **Journaling:** Regular journaling can be a powerful tool for self-discovery. Write about your aspirations, fears, successes, and failures. Reflect on how your business activities resonate with your inner self. Journaling offers clarity and insight into your spiritual motivations.

> **Value Identification:** Make a list of values that are important to you personally and professionally. Rank these values in order of importance. Reflect on how these values are (or are not) expressed in your current business practices. This exercise helps in aligning your business operations with your core values.

> **Life Purpose Statement:** Write a statement that encapsulates your life's purpose. Consider how your business endeavours contribute to this purpose. This exercise fosters a deeper understanding of how your business activities fit into your larger life goals.

The Role of Meditation and Mindfulness in Self-Discovery

Meditation and mindfulness are powerful practices for self-reflection and discovery. These practices help quiet the mind, allowing deeper insights and intuitions to surface. They offer a space to detach from daily business stress and connect with your inner self.

Meditation can be particularly effective in uncovering spiritual motivations. Through meditation, you can explore your inner landscape, free from the distractions of the external world. This exploration can lead to profound insights about what truly drives you in your business endeavours.

Mindfulness, on the other hand, is about being present and fully engaged in the moment. It can be practised throughout the day, not just in quiet contemplation. Mindful entrepreneurship means being conscious of your thoughts, actions, and decisions and how they align with your spiritual motivations.

Balancing the Inner and Outer Journey of Entrepreneurship

The entrepreneurial journey is a balance of external success and internal fulfilment. While external success is measured in business growth and profitability, internal fulfilment is how well your business aligns with your spiritual motivations.

Balancing these two aspects requires regular self-reflection and mindfulness. It involves continually returning to your core values and purpose, ensuring that your business decisions and actions harmonise with them. This balance is not static but a dynamic process that evolves as you and your business grow.

One of the challenges in maintaining a connection to your spiritual motivations is the fast-paced and often stressful nature of entrepreneurship. In pursuing business goals, losing sight of your deeper motivations is easy.

Another challenge is the pressure to conform to conventional business norms and practices, which may not always align with your spiritual values. It requires courage and resilience to stay true to your values in the face of external pressures.

Strategies for Staying Connected to Your Spiritual Self

Regular Self-Reflection: Make self-reflection a regular practice. Set aside weekly time to reflect on your business activities and how they align with your spiritual motivations.

Mindful Decision-Making: Incorporate mindfulness into your decision-making process. Before making business decisions, pause and reflect on how these decisions align with your values and life purpose.

Seeking Support: Surround yourself with mentors, advisors, or a community that understands and supports your approach to spiritually motivated entrepreneurship.

Adaptation and Flexibility: Be open to adapting your business practices as you grow and learn. Your understanding of your spiritual motivations may evolve, and your business practices should reflect this evolution.

Integrating your spiritual motivations into your business is not just about big strategic decisions; it's also about the day-to-day operations. It's about treating your employees, interacting with your customers, and engaging with your community. It's about your products or services and how you market them.

This integration is an ongoing process, one that requires constant attention and intention. It's about making your business reflect your inner self, manifesting your deepest values and beliefs.

You unlock a transformative power by aligning your business with your spiritual motivations. Your business becomes more than just a means to make a living; it becomes a vehicle for expressing your deepest self, making a positive impact, and contributing to the greater good.

This alignment leads to not just external success but also internal fulfilment. It brings a sense of purpose and meaning to your entrepreneurial journey, making it more rewarding and sustainable in the long run.

Embarking on a journey of self-reflection and discovery is essential for any entrepreneur who seeks to align their business with their spiritual motivations. It's a journey that requires courage, honesty, and commitment. But the rewards –personal fulfilment, meaningful impact, and sustainable success – are immeasurable. By staying connected to your spiritual motivations, you create a successful business and a true reflection of who you are and what you believe in.

Challenges of Staying True to Spiritual Motivations

In pursuing spirituality in business practices, entrepreneurs often find themselves at a crossroads where their spiritual motivations and the practical demands of running a business seem to be at odds. This article explores the challenges of maintaining spiritual integrity in business and guides navigating these waters while staying true to one's spiritual core.

The journey of aligning business with spirituality is not a straightforward path. It is filled with complexities and challenges that test the entrepreneur's commitment to their spiritual motivations. Understanding these challenges is the first step in developing strategies to overcome them.

Navigating Market Pressures

One of the primary challenges spiritually-motivated entrepreneurs face is the pressure of the market. The business world is competitively driven by profit and growth. This often clashes with the spiritual values of compassion, mindfulness, and ethical practices. Entrepreneurs may be pressured to compromise on their values to stay competitive or meet market expectations.

Managing Financial Constraints

Financial constraints are a reality for most businesses, especially startups and small enterprises. Balancing the budget while making decisions aligned with spiritual values can be challenging. For example, sourcing ethically produced materials or paying fair wages can increase costs, impacting the business's financial viability.

Ethical Dilemmas and Decision Making

Entrepreneurs are frequently faced with decisions that pose ethical dilemmas. These dilemmas can be particularly challenging when they conflict between business interests and spiritual values. Decisions such as layoffs, pricing strategies, or business partnerships often require navigating complex ethical terrains.

Maintaining Spiritual Integrity Amidst Challenges

While these challenges can be daunting, there are ways to maintain spiritual integrity and resilience in the face of them.

> **Embracing Mindfulness and Reflection**: Regular mindfulness practices can help entrepreneurs stay grounded in their values. Reflection on one's actions and decisions ensures that they align with spiritual motivations.

> **Building a Supportive Community:** Surrounding oneself with like-minded individuals, mentors, or a community that shares similar values can provide support and guidance.

This community can offer different perspectives and solutions to challenges faced in the business world.

Prioritizing Ethical Decision Making: Making ethics a priority in every business decision can help maintain spiritual integrity. This involves assessing the impact of each decision on stakeholders and the environment and choosing the option that aligns best with spiritual values.

Transparent Communication: Being transparent with stakeholders about the spiritual motivations behind the business and the challenges faced can build trust and understanding. This transparency can also attract customers and partners who share similar values.

Adaptability and Creative Problem Solving: Adaptability and openness to creative solutions can help entrepreneurs navigate financial and market pressures without compromising their spiritual values. This might involve innovative business models, alternative funding sources, or unique marketing strategies.

Balancing Pragmatism and Idealism: Balancing the idealism of spiritual motivations with the pragmatism of running a business is crucial. This balance involves making practical decisions that do not stray far from core values.

Developing Resilience: Building resilience to withstand challenges is essential. Resilience can be fostered through regular self-care practices, maintaining a positive outlook, and learning from failures and setbacks.

Real-Life Examples of Overcoming Challenges

Many entrepreneurs have successfully navigated these challenges while staying true to their spiritual motivations. For example, a business that chooses to source materials ethically might find innovative ways to reduce costs in other areas or create a unique brand story that attracts a niche market willing to pay a premium. Another example is a business facing financial constraints that chooses to adopt a lean business model that focuses on quality and ethics rather than rapid growth.

Integrating Spiritual Practices into Business Operations

Integrating spiritual practices such as meditation, mindfulness, or regular retreats into business operations can help maintain a connection to spiritual motivations. These practices can clarify, reduce stress, and foster a work culture reflecting the entrepreneur's spiritual values.

The Role of Leadership in Overcoming Challenges

Leadership plays a crucial role in overcoming these challenges. A leader who embodies the spiritual values of the business can inspire employees, build a strong company culture, and make decisions that reflect these values. This leadership involves leading by example, being empathetic, and communicating effectively.

Future Outlook and Continuous Growth

Maintaining spiritual integrity in business is an ongoing process. It requires continuous self-reflection, learning, and growth. As the business environment and individual spirituality evolve, so too must the strategies to align them.

Empowering Others Through Spiritual Entrepreneurship

Entrepreneurs who successfully navigate these challenges can serve as role models and inspire others. They can demonstrate that it is possible to run a successful business while staying true to spiritual values, thereby contributing to a shift in the business paradigm towards more ethical and conscious practices.

The challenges of aligning business practices with spiritual motivations are significant but not insurmountable. Entrepreneurs can navigate these challenges effectively with mindfulness, resilience, adaptability, and a commitment to ethical decision-making. By doing so, they build successful businesses and contribute to a more conscious and value-driven business world. As they journey through the complexities of entrepreneurship, their spiritual motivations become a beacon, guiding them towards business success, personal fulfilment, and a positive impact on the world.

Ch 2. Vision and Values
Aligning your business with your spiritual beliefs.

In the heart of every business lies a core set of values and a vision that transcends the daily grind of commerce. These are not just abstract concepts; they are the guiding stars that shape decisions, define culture, and ultimately determine the impact of a business in the world. In this chapter, "Vision and Values: Aligning Your Business with Your Spiritual Beliefs," we delve into the profound connection between your deepest spiritual beliefs and how they can inform and direct your business practices.

Entrepreneurship is more than merely exchanging goods and services; it reflects one's inner world and manifests personal beliefs and values. When these intrinsic elements align with your business operations, the journey transcends the traditional success metrics, offering a profound and rewarding sense of fulfilment.

The Essence of Spiritual Beliefs in Business

At its core, aligning your business with your spiritual beliefs means weaving your values and ethos into the fabric of your professional endeavours. This alignment is not just about ethical business practices; it's about creating a business that is a true reflection of your inner self. It's about ensuring every decision, from product development to customer service, resonates with your spiritual compass.

Your business vision is not just a statement; it's a declaration of purpose. This chapter guides you through crafting a vision deeply imbued with your spiritual values. It's about envisioning a future where your business thrives financially and contributes positively to the collective well-being, staying true to the principles that matter most to you.

Understanding your spiritual values is one thing; integrating them into your business is another. This chapter section focuses on translating spiritual values into tangible business practices. Whether through ethical sourcing, mindful leadership, or community engagement, we explore ways to make your values a living, breathing part of your business operations.

Aligning your business with your spiritual beliefs is a journey fraught with challenges. This chapter does not shy away from discussing the potential conflicts and dilemmas that might arise and offers strategies to navigate these complexities. It's about balancing spiritual ideals and business operations' practical realities.

This chapter invites you to embark on a transformative journey where your business becomes a vessel for your spiritual expression. It's about creating a legacy that reflects economic success and a deeper fulfilment and contribution to the world. As we delve into the nuances of aligning your business with your spiritual beliefs, remember that this path of continuous learning and evolution promises to enrich your business and your entire life.

Defining Your Spiritual Compass

In aligning your business with your spiritual ethos, the first crucial step is to define your spiritual compass – that is, to identify and articulate your core beliefs and values. This process is deeply personal and reflective, involving introspection and a willingness to explore the depths of your spiritual identity. This article guides you through this transformative process, presenting exercises, questions, and case studies to aid in discovering the spiritual underpinnings that can serve as the foundation for your business.

Before delving into identifying your spiritual compass, it's essential to understand the role these beliefs play in business. Your spiritual beliefs and values are not just personal guiding principles; they can significantly influence your business ethics, decision-making processes, leadership style, and overall approach to your entrepreneurial journey. They can imbue your business practices with a sense of purpose and meaning that goes beyond the pursuit of profit.

The Process of Identifying Core Beliefs and Values

> **Self-Reflection and Meditation:** Begin with introspective practices like meditation or mindfulness to clear your mind and focus on your inner self. These practices can provide clarity and calm, setting the right tone for deep self-reflection. During meditation, ask yourself what values

resonate deeply with you. Consider what principles you find non-negotiable in life and business.

Journaling and Articulation: Journaling is a powerful tool for articulation. Write about experiences that have shaped your beliefs, moments of clarity about what matters to you, and how you see these reflections playing a role in your business. Consider prompts such as "What principles do I want my business to embody?" or "How do my spiritual beliefs influence my view of success?"

Historical and Cultural Reflection: Reflect on your cultural, historical, and family background. Often, our core beliefs are shaped by our upbringing and cultural experiences. Acknowledge how these influences contribute to your spiritual outlook and how they can be integrated into your business philosophy.

Ethical and Moral Considerations: Think about ethical and moral dilemmas you have faced and how you resolved them. These scenarios can reveal a lot about your core values and how you might handle similar situations in business.

Exercises for Uncovering Your Spiritual Compass

Value Sorting Exercise: Create a list of values and sort them according to their importance to you. This exercise helps prioritise your values and understand which ones are non-negotiable in your business.

Vision Board Creation: Develop a vision board that represents your spiritual values and beliefs. Use images, words, and symbols to represent your spiritual compass visually.

Role Model Reflection: Identify individuals who embody the values you admire. Reflect on what aspects of their character and actions resonate with you and how these traits can be emulated in your business.

Crafting a Spiritually Aligned Vision Statement

Once you clearly understand your core spiritual beliefs and values, the next step is to craft a vision statement for your business that aligns with these principles.

Integrating Values into Your Vision Statement: Your vision statement should clearly and concisely reflect your core beliefs and values. It should articulate what you want to achieve with your business and how you plan to achieve it in alignment with your spiritual compass.

Ensuring Clarity and Authenticity: The vision statement should be clear, authentic, and inspiring. It should resonate with you and your team and guide all your business activities.

Flexibility and Evolution: Be open to the evolution of your vision statement. As you grow in your spiritual and entrepreneurial journey, your vision may evolve to reflect deeper understandings and insights.

Real-World Examples and Case Studies

The article can benefit from incorporating case studies of businesses and entrepreneurs who have successfully aligned their operations with their spiritual beliefs. These real-world examples can provide practical insights and inspiration for readers.

Incorporating Diverse Spiritual Practices

Respect and inclusivity for diverse spiritual beliefs are crucial. This article should cover a range of beliefs and practices, illustrating how different spiritual paths can be integrated into business.

Challenges and Overcoming Them

Identifying and integrating your spiritual beliefs into your business is not without challenges. The article can discuss common obstacles like societal pressures, market demands, and internal conflicts, offering guidance on how to stay true to your spiritual compass amidst these challenges.

Defining your spiritual compass is a journey of self-discovery that requires honesty, introspection, and a commitment to living your values. By identifying your core beliefs and values and crafting a vision statement that aligns with these principles, you set the foundation for a business that is not only successful in conventional terms but also a true reflection of your spiritual identity. This alignment paves the way for a fulfilling entrepreneurial journey, rooted in integrity and purpose.

Crafting a Spiritually Aligned Vision Statement for Your Business

In the landscape of modern entrepreneurship, a vision statement is not just a corporate formalism; it's the soul of a business, encapsulating its aspirations, ethos, and core principles. When this vision statement is infused with an entrepreneur's spiritual values, it transforms into a guiding light that illuminates the entire business journey. This article provides a comprehensive guide on developing a vision statement that mirrors your spiritual values and illustrates how to implement these values into your business practices, supported by inspiring examples from successful businesses.

Understanding the Importance of a Spiritually-Aligned Vision Statement

A spiritually aligned vision statement serves as a compass, directing every aspect of a business's operations, strategies, and decision-making processes. It acts as a constant reminder of why the business exists and what it aspires to achieve beyond financial success. This alignment ensures that the business thrives in the marketplace and fosters spiritual fulfilment for the entrepreneur, employees, and the community it serves.

The Process of Crafting Your Vision Statement

1. **Reflect on Your Spiritual Values:** Start by identifying the spiritual values that are most important to you. These could be principles derived from your faith, personal beliefs, or life experiences. Reflect on how these values shape your view of the world and what you want to contribute through your business.

2. **Translate Values into Business Language:** Consider how your spiritual values can be translated into the language of business. For instance, if one of your core values is

compassion, consider how this can influence your business practices, customer relations, and community engagement.

3. **Envision the Impact:** Visualize the impact you want your business to have. How do your spiritual values inform this vision? This could range from creating an inclusive work culture to engaging in sustainable practices or contributing to social causes.

4. **Drafting the Statement:** Begin drafting your vision statement. Keep it concise, clear, and inspirational. It should resonate with everyone interacting with your business, from employees to customers.

5. **Seek Feedback and Refine:** Share your draft with trusted advisors, mentors, or colleagues. Seek feedback and be open to refining your statement to ensure it accurately reflects your spiritual values and business aspirations.

Examples of Spiritually Aligned Vision Statements

1. **A Sustainable Fashion Brand:** To revolutionize the fashion industry by championing sustainable practices and celebrating ethical elegance, embodying the spiritual principle of stewardship for the Earth in every garment we create.

2. **A Health and Wellness Company:** To enhance the wellbeing of individuals and communities through holistic health solutions, rooted in our commitment to the spiritual value of nurturing mind, body, and soul.

3. **A Technology Firm:** To innovate for a better tomorrow, leveraging technology to create solutions that honor our spiritual commitment to connectivity, accessibility, and ethical progress.

Implementing Values into Business Practices.

1. **Embedding Values in Corporate Culture:** Ensure that your spiritual values are reflected in your company's culture. This can involve creating policies and practices that promote these values, such as diversity and inclusion initiatives, ethical sourcing, or environmentally friendly operations.

2. **Decision Making Aligned with Spiritual Values:** Use your vision statement as a filter for all business decisions. Before making any significant decision, ask whether it aligns with your vision and values. This alignment ensures consistency and integrity in all business activities.

3. **Training and Development:** Invest in training and development programs that reinforce your spiritual values among your employees. Encourage them to find ways to incorporate these values into their work.

4. **Community Engagement and Social Responsibility:** Engage in community initiatives and social responsibility projects that reflect your spiritual values. This helps give back to the community and strengthens your brand's identity and loyalty among customers.

Regular Assessment and Adaptation: Regularly assess how well your business practices align with your spiritual values. Be open to making adjustments as your business evolves.

Crafting a vision statement that reflects your spiritual values and implementing these principles into your business practices is a journey of continuous growth and alignment. It requires introspection, commitment, and a willingness to stand by your values in every aspect of your business. By doing so, you create a business that is not just successful in the conventional sense but is also a true reflection of your spiritual ethos, contributing positively to the world and leaving a lasting legacy.

Integrating Spiritual Values into Everyday Business Operations

In an era where business is often driven by profit and competition, integrating spiritual values into everyday operations presents a refreshing paradigm shift. This approach redefines success and ensures that the company contributes positively to society and the environment, adhering to a higher ethical standard. This article explores the practical ways businesses can integrate spiritual values into their operations, overcome common challenges, and measure success from a spiritual perspective.

The Essence of Spiritual Values in Business

Incorporating spiritual values into business practices goes beyond mere ethical compliance; it involves a deeper commitment to principles that elevate both the individual and collective well-being. These values often stem from personal beliefs, cultural traditions, or religious teachings, including integrity, compassion, stewardship, and community. When businesses align their operations with such values, they create a positive impact that transcends financial gains.

Ethical decision-making is the cornerstone of integrating spiritual values into business operations. It involves considering the impact of every decision on all stakeholders, including employees, customers, suppliers, and the environment. Ethical decision-making requires a commitment to transparency, honesty, and fairness, even when faced with choices that might be financially less advantageous.

For instance, a business might choose to source materials from suppliers who uphold fair labour practices, even if it means higher costs. Such decisions reinforce the commitment to ethical practices and resonate with customers who value social responsibility, ultimately leading to long-term loyalty and trust.

A values-driven work culture reflects the company's spiritual values in every aspect of its operations. This involves not just adherence to ethical practices but also fostering a work environment that respects diversity, encourages personal growth, and promotes a sense of community.

Building such a culture starts with leadership. Leaders who embody the company's spiritual values set a precedent for the rest of the organization. They must lead by example, demonstrating through their actions and decisions that the company's values are non-negotiable.

In addition, regular training and development programs can help employees understand and embrace these values. Creating platforms where employees can share their experiences and ideas on integrating these values further enriches the culture.

Customer relationships based on spiritual values are built on trust, respect, and a genuine concern for the customer's well-being. This means going beyond the transactional nature of business and engaging with customers in a way that reflects the company's core values.

For instance, a business that values compassion might implement policies that ensure customer satisfaction, such as fair return policies or personalized customer service. Such practices enhance customer loyalty and reinforce the company's commitment to its values.

Environmental stewardship is a critical aspect of many spiritual traditions. Businesses can integrate this value by adopting sustainable practices. This might include using eco-friendly materials, minimizing waste, or investing in renewable energy.

Sustainable practices often require upfront investment and a long-term view, which can be challenging in a profit-driven business environment. However, the long-term benefits, including cost savings, improved brand reputation, and compliance with environmental regulations, can outweigh these initial challenges.

Maintaining value alignment in a competitive business environment is fraught with challenges. The pressure to cut costs, increase profits, and stay ahead of competitors can sometimes conflict with the company's spiritual values.

To overcome these challenges, businesses must clearly understand their core values and a strong commitment to uphold them. This might involve making difficult decisions that favor values over short-term gains.

Moreover, businesses must be adaptable, finding innovative ways to integrate their values while remaining competitive. This could involve exploring new business models, diversifying products or services, or finding niche markets where their values are a unique selling proposition.

Measuring success in a spiritually-aligned business goes beyond financial metrics. While profitability is important, companies must also consider the impact of their operations on society and the environment.

This might involve measuring customer satisfaction, employee engagement, environmental impact, or community involvement. Businesses can develop their own metrics or adopt existing frameworks such as the Triple Bottom Line, which evaluates a company's social, environmental, and financial performance.

Success from a spiritual perspective is about creating a balance between financial viability and the fulfilment of the company's spiritual values. It's about building a business that thrives economically and contributes positively to the world.

Incorporating spiritual values into everyday business operations presents a holistic approach to entrepreneurship. It challenges the traditional success metrics, placing equal importance on ethical practices, community well-being, and environmental stewardship. While integrating these values can be challenging, the long-term benefits of building a business that is aligned with one's spiritual beliefs are immeasurable. This approach fosters a positive impact on society and the environment and ensures that the business remains true to its core values, creating a legacy that extends beyond financial success.

Redefining Business Success: Embracing Spiritual and Ethical Metrics

In the contemporary business landscape, success is often quantified regarding financial achievements – profit margins, market share, and return on investment. However, for businesses guided by spiritual values, the definition of success encompasses much more. It involves positively impacting the world, fostering employee well-being, practising environmental stewardship, and actively engaging with the community. This article delves into the alternative metrics for measuring business success aligned with spiritual values, offering tools and methodologies to assess both the spiritual and ethical impact alongside financial health.

The Shift in Success Metrics

The traditional business model, primarily focused on financial gain, has led to many challenges, including environmental degradation, employee burnout, and social inequalities. Businesses driven by spiritual values are leading a shift towards a more holistic approach to success. This approach considers the well-being of all stakeholders – employees, customers, society, and the environment.

Employee Well-Being as a Measure of Success

One of the primary indicators of a spiritually-aligned business is the well-being of its employees. A business embodying spiritual values creates a work environment where employees feel valued, respected, and part of a greater mission. Metrics for measuring employee well-being include:

Employee Satisfaction Surveys: Regular surveys can gauge employees' happiness, fulfilment, and alignment with the company's values.

Turnover Rates: A lower turnover rate can indicate a healthy work environment, while a higher rate might suggest areas needing improvement.

Employee Development: Investment in employee growth and development clearly indicates a company's commitment to its workforce.

Environmental Stewardship: Going Beyond Profit

Environmental stewardship is a critical aspect of spiritually-aligned businesses. Metrics in this area are about compliance and actively contributing to environmental sustainability. They include:

Carbon Footprint Assessment: Regularly measure the company's carbon footprint to minimise it.

Sustainable Practices: Adopting and reporting sustainable production, sourcing, and distribution practices.

Waste Reduction: Metrics that track waste reduction and improvement in recycling efforts.

Community Engagement and Social Impact

A spiritually-aligned business views success through its positive impact on society. This involves engaging with the community and contributing to social causes. Metrics for community engagement and social impact might include:

Community Initiatives: Active participation in community service or social cause initiatives.

Social Impact Assessments: Evaluate how the business's operations positively affect the community.

Partnerships with Non-Profits: Collaborations with non-profit organizations for societal betterment.

Tools and Methodologies for Assessing Spiritual and Ethical Impact

Measuring a business's spiritual and ethical impact requires a combination of qualitative and quantitative tools. A few of the following methods can be employed:

Triple Bottom Line: This framework expands the traditional reporting framework to include social and environmental (or ecological) parameters alongside financial ones. The TBL framework encourages businesses to regard social and ecological impacts as a performance measure.

Ethical Audits: Regular ethical audits can help assess the company's operations in light of its spiritual and moral values. These audits can cover areas like fair labour practices, ethical sourcing, and corporate governance.

Stakeholder Feedback: Gathering feedback from all stakeholders, including employees, customers, suppliers, and community members, offers insights into the company's ethical and spiritual impact.

Sustainability Reporting: Adopting standards like the Global Reporting Initiative (GRI) for sustainability reporting can help businesses measure their environmental and social impact.

Balancing Financial Health with Spiritual and Ethical Metrics

While embracing spiritual and ethical metrics, businesses must also maintain financial health. This balance is crucial for the sustainability of the company. Tools like balanced scorecards can help keep this balance, ensuring financial objectives do not overshadow spiritual and ethical goals.

Employee Engagement and Spirituality

Employee engagement goes beyond job satisfaction; it also involves connecting employees with the company's spiritual values. This can be achieved through regular workshops, retreats, and team-building exercises focused on the company's values.

Leadership plays a crucial role in implementing and maintaining these alternative success metrics. Mindful leadership, focused on self-awareness, empathy, and a deep understanding of the company's spiritual values, can inspire and guide employees towards its holistic goals.

Integrating spiritual values into business practices and adopting alternative metrics for measuring success represents a transformative shift in the business world. This shift challenges traditional notions of success and opens up new avenues for businesses to positively impact society and the environment. By adopting these alternative metrics, businesses can balance financial viability and their commitment to spiritual and ethical principles. This approach leads to a more sustainable, equitable, and compassionate world where businesses are a force for good, contributing to the overall well-being of all stakeholders.

Ch 3. Mindful Planning
Creating a business plan that reflects your values

Embarking on the entrepreneurial journey is akin to setting sail on a vast, uncharted ocean. Your business plan is your compass, guiding you through tumultuous markets and shifting trends. But what if this compass could be aligned with the stars of profit and growth and the deeper, more enduring lights of your spiritual values? This chapter, "Mindful Planning: Creating a Business Plan That Reflects Your Values," is dedicated to intertwining the pragmatism of business planning with the profound principles of your spiritual beliefs.

The Essence of a Value-Driven Business Plan

A business plan, in its traditional sense, lays out a business's objectives, strategies, market analysis, and financial forecasts. However, when it is imbued with your personal values, it transcends these elements, becoming a living document that charts a course for economic success, spiritual fulfilment, and ethical impact. This integration of values into your business plan declares that your venture isn't just about what you do, but also about who you are and what you stand for.

The Journey of Integrating Values into Your Business Plan

Infusing your business plan with your spiritual values begins with deep introspection. It involves a thoughtful examination of what these values are, how they have shaped your life, and how they can be woven seamlessly into the fabric of your business. This introspective journey challenges you to understand your values and live them through every aspect of your business.

The first step in this journey is to align your spiritual values with your business goals. This alignment is about ensuring that your pursuit of commercial success does not stray from your ethical and spiritual principles. For instance, if one of your core values is compassion, how does that reflect in your business objectives? Does it mean prioritizing employee welfare, engaging in fair trade practices, or maybe focusing on products and services that contribute positively to society?

With your goals aligned with your values, the next step is to embed these values into your business strategies and operations. This integration is what differentiates a value-driven business plan from a conventional one. It influences your choice of suppliers, marketing approach, customer service ethos, and operational decisions. This chapter will delve into practical strategies for making your values an integral part of your business operations, ensuring that every decision and action reflects your spiritual ethos.

One of the most significant challenges in creating a business plan that reflects your values is ensuring that these principles are more than just words on paper. They need to be lived and be breathed, becoming a part of the DNA of your company.

In a value-driven business plan, success is measured by financial metrics and how well the business upholds its spiritual values. This chapter will introduce you to alternative success metrics, including social impact, environmental stewardship, employee satisfaction, and community engagement. It will guide you on how to set up systems and processes to measure these non-financial aspects of success, ensuring that your business remains true to its spiritual core.

To inspire and guide you, this chapter will also feature real-world examples of businesses that have successfully integrated their spiritual values into their business plans. These case studies will illustrate the challenges and triumphs of aligning a business with spiritual values and provide practical insights you can apply to your venture.

Creating a business plan that reflects your values involves aligning your entrepreneurial aspirations with your spiritual ethos. It's about building a business that not only seeks to be profitable but also strives to make a positive impact on the world. This chapter will provide you with the tools, insights, and inspiration to craft a business plan that truly reflects your values, guiding you to build a business that is not just successful in the traditional sense but also rich in spiritual fulfilment and ethical integrity.

Integrating Spiritual Values into Business Objectives

In a world where business is often synonymous with financial gain, integrating spiritual values into business objectives presents an enlightening shift in perspective. This approach does not merely focus on profit margins but emphasizes a deeper, more fulfilling sense of purpose. This article explores how entrepreneurs can infuse their core spiritual values into the objectives of their business, guiding them to set goals that are not only financially viable but also spiritually enriching.

Integrating spiritual values into business objectives is a transformative process that begins with recognizing that a business can be an extension of one's personal beliefs and values. It's about seeing your business as a platform to manifest your spiritual principles, whether rooted in mindfulness, stewardship, compassion, or any other deeply held belief.

Before integrating spiritual values into your business objectives, it's essential to understand what these values represent for you. Spiritual values can range from a commitment to ethical practices and social responsibility to fostering well-being and harmony. They can also include environmental consciousness, community service, and promoting fairness and equality.

The first step in this integration process is a reflective one. Entrepreneurs must delve into their spiritual beliefs to understand what truly matters to them. This can be achieved through meditation, journaling, or any practice allowing deep introspection. The goal is to identify the core spiritual values you wish to see mirrored in your business.

Once these values are identified, the next step is to translate them into tangible business objectives. This translation involves looking at each aspect of the business through the lens of your spiritual values. For instance, if environmental stewardship is a core value, a business goal could be to minimize your operations' environmental footprint or offer eco-friendly products.

Setting spiritually-aligned business goals requires a balance between financial viability and spiritual fulfilment. It's about defining success in broader terms than just profit. These goals should also be SMART

– Specific, Measurable, Achievable, Relevant, and Time-bound – but with the added dimension of spiritual alignment.

A business's mission and vision statements are ideal places to integrate spiritual values. These statements should reflect what the business aims to achieve and how it plans to achieve these objectives in a way that aligns with the entrepreneur's spiritual beliefs.

Beyond the mission and vision, spiritual values should be evident in the business's day-to-day operations. This could mean creating a workplace culture that promotes employee well-being, adopting sustainable business practices, or ensuring that your supply chain adheres to ethical standards.

Integrating spiritual values into business objectives is not without its challenges. There can be a perceived conflict between profitability and maintaining spiritual integrity. Overcoming these challenges involves creativity, innovation, and a commitment to finding solutions that uphold your spiritual values without compromising business viability.

There are numerous examples of businesses successfully integrating spiritual values into their objectives. These businesses span various industries but share a joint commitment to operating in a manner that reflects their spiritual beliefs. Examples include companies focusing on sustainability, those creating inclusive work environments, and businesses prioritizing ethical sourcing and fair trade practices.

Leadership plays a crucial role in this integration process. Leaders must embody the business's spiritual values and inspire their teams to do the same. This involves leading by example, open communication, and creating an environment where spiritual values are respected and encouraged.

Measuring the impact of spiritual values on business objectives involves looking at both quantitative and qualitative indicators. This could include measuring employee satisfaction, customer loyalty, the environmental impact of the business, and the business's contribution to the community.

One of the critical aspects of integrating spiritual values into business objectives is maintaining a balance between these values and the realities of the market. This balance requires a nuanced understanding of navigating the business landscape while staying true to your spiritual principles.

Integrating spiritual values into business objectives is a journey that transforms the way we view and conduct business. It's about creating a company that not only achieves financial success but also contributes positively to society and aligns with the more profound spiritual beliefs of the entrepreneur. This approach to business planning creates a more fulfilling and meaningful entrepreneurial journey, where success is measured not just in financial terms but in the business's positive impact on the world.

Ethical Frameworks in Decision-Making

In the intricate tapestry of business, ethical frameworks in decision-making stand as the threads that hold the moral fabric of a company together. Far beyond the pursuit of profit, these frameworks guide businesses in navigating the complex landscape of modern commerce with integrity and purpose. The importance of incorporating ethical frameworks in business decision-making processes, particularly for those entrepreneurs who seek alignment with their spiritual values, cannot be overstressed. This article will explore the nuances of creating ethical decision-making guidelines that resonate with an entrepreneur's spiritual ethos, touching upon ethical sourcing, conscious marketing, equitable employment practices, and environmentally responsible operations. Additionally, it will shed light on the challenges of upholding ethical integrity in a competitive market and strategies to surmount these hurdles.

At the heart of ethical decision-making in business lies the principle of doing what is right, not just what is profitable or convenient. This principle is especially significant for entrepreneurs who consider their business as an extension of their spiritual journey. For them, decisions are not merely transactional but testaments to their values and beliefs. Ethical frameworks in business decision-making serve as a compass that guides these entrepreneurs, ensuring that every choice, big or small, aligns with their spiritual and moral convictions.

Creating such ethical frameworks begins with deeply understanding one's spiritual values. These values could range from honesty and fairness to compassion and stewardship. The key is clearly defining these values and then articulating how they translate into business practices. This translation is not always straightforward, as the business world often presents complex ethical dilemmas. However, with well-defined values, entrepreneurs can navigate these dilemmas with clarity and conviction.

Ethical sourcing is one of the pillars of an ethical decision-making framework. It involves choosing suppliers and materials that align with the company's values. For instance, a business committed to environmental stewardship might opt for suppliers who use sustainable practices, even if their costs are higher. Similarly, a company valuing human dignity would avoid suppliers implicated in unfair labour practices. Ethical sourcing, while morally commendable, can present challenges, particularly in industries where cost competition is fierce. However, the long-term benefits of brand loyalty, customer trust, and alignment with personal values often outweigh these challenges.

Conscious marketing is another aspect where ethical frameworks play a crucial role. This marketing approach emphasizes transparency, honesty, and respect for the consumer. It shuns manipulative tactics and exaggerated claims, focusing instead on building genuine customer relationships. Conscious marketing not only reflects the spiritual values of the entrepreneur but also fosters a deeper connection with the customer base. The challenge here is balancing creativity and persuasion with honesty and integrity, a task that requires skill and commitment.

Equitable employment practices are a testament to a company's ethical framework. This involves fair hiring practices, providing a safe and respectful work environment, and ensuring that employees are valued and treated justly. For a spiritually inclined entrepreneur, employees are not just workers but fellow beings on a shared journey. Thus, their well-being becomes a paramount concern. The challenge in maintaining equitable employment practices often arises in balancing profitability with fairness, especially for small businesses or startups. However, employee investment often pays off in terms of loyalty, productivity, and a positive company culture.

Environmentally responsible operations are increasingly becoming a cornerstone of ethical business practices. This involves minimizing the environmental impact of the business, using resources sustainably, and actively contributing to environmental conservation. This aspect of their ethical framework is non-negotiable for entrepreneurs whose spiritual values include stewardship of the Earth. The challenge lies in finding environmentally friendly options that do not compromise the business's financial viability. However, this challenge is becoming more manageable with growing consumer awareness and preference for eco-friendly businesses.

Upholding ethical integrity in a competitive market is a significant challenge. The pressure to cut costs, increase market share, and stay ahead of competitors can sometimes push businesses to compromise on their values. The key to overcoming this challenge is resilience and a long-term view of success. Companies that stay true to their ethical frameworks often build stronger, more loyal customer bases and create a unique space for themselves in the market. They also attract employees who share their values, creating a workforce motivated by salaries and a shared sense of purpose.

In addition to resilience, creativity and innovation are crucial in maintaining ethical integrity. This might involve exploring new business models, finding niche markets, or using technology to reduce costs without compromising on values. Networking with like-minded businesses and participating in forums focused on ethical practices can also provide support and ideas.

Incorporating ethical frameworks into business decision-making is more than a strategy; it is a commitment to a way of doing business that honours one's spiritual values. It is a journey fraught with challenges and opportunities to impact the world positively. As companies increasingly recognize the importance of ethics and spirituality in their operations, the commerce landscape is slowly but surely transforming into one that values profit, purpose, integrity, and responsibility.

Ethical frameworks in business are not just about adhering to laws and regulations; they represent a conscious choice to infuse every business activity with integrity and purpose. For entrepreneurs who hold their spiritual values close, these frameworks are a means to ensure their business actions reflect their deepest convictions. Integrating these frameworks is multifaceted, involving introspection, goal-setting, and a steadfast commitment to uphold these values in the face of market pressures.

Understanding the Ethical Implications of Business Decisions

In the realm of business, every decision carries ethical implications. From how a company treats its employees and interacts with customers to how it sources materials and manages its environmental footprint, each aspect of business operations can reflect the entrepreneur's spiritual and ethical stance. The challenge lies in making decisions that balance profitability with these ethical considerations.

Setting Spiritual and Ethical Goals

The journey begins with setting goals that are not just business-oriented but also spiritually and ethically driven. This might involve committing to sustainable business practices, ensuring fairness in all dealings, or dedicating a portion of the company's efforts to social causes. These goals serve as a north star, guiding the entrepreneur through the complexities of business operations while keeping their spiritual values in focus.

Creating Ethical Guidelines for Decision-Making

One practical approach is to develop a set of ethical guidelines that serve as a reference for all business decisions. These guidelines should reflect the entrepreneur's spiritual values, translated into the context of business operations. They should cover various aspects of the business, from ethical sourcing and sustainable practices to employee relations and customer engagement.

Ethical Sourcing and Supply Chain Integrity

Ethical sourcing is critical to these frameworks, particularly for businesses committed to spiritual values like stewardship and compassion. This involves ensuring that every component of the product or service is obtained in a way that aligns with these values. It might mean choosing suppliers who adhere to fair labour practices or opting for environmentally sustainable materials.

Implementing Conscious Marketing Practices

In marketing, applying ethical frameworks involves a commitment to transparency and honesty. This means avoiding misleading advertisements or hyperbolic claims and instead focusing on building genuine customer relationships based on trust and respect.

Conscious marketing aligns with spiritual values and fosters long-term customer loyalty.

Fostering Equitable Employment Practices

Equitable employment practices are another area where ethical frameworks play a vital role. This involves creating a workplace that respects diversity, values each employee, and promotes a culture of inclusion and fairness. By aligning employment practices with spiritual values, businesses can create a motivated, loyal, and productive workforce.

Adopting Environmentally Responsible Operations

Environmentally responsible operations are crucial for businesses aligning with spiritual values of stewardship and responsibility. This can include reducing waste, minimizing carbon footprint, and using renewable resources. While these practices might require initial investment and a shift in operations, they contribute to a sustainable future and resonate deeply with customers who share these values.

Overcoming Challenges in Ethical Decision-Making

One of the significant challenges in this journey is maintaining these ethical standards in a competitive and often cutthroat market. It requires resilience and a commitment to not compromise on these core values for short-term gains. It also involves educating customers and stakeholders about the value and importance of these ethical practices, which can create a supportive and engaged community around the business.

Strategies for Upholding Ethical Integrity

Upholding ethical integrity amid market pressures often requires innovative thinking and strategic planning. This might involve finding niche markets where customers value ethical practices, forming alliances with like-minded businesses, or leveraging technology to reduce costs while maintaining ethical standards.

Measuring Success Through an Ethical Lens

Finally, measuring success in a business driven by spiritual and ethical values requires a broader perspective. Beyond financial metrics, this includes assessing the impact on employees, the environment, and the community. It involves regular reflection and assessment to ensure that the business stays true to its ethical and spiritual objectives.

In essence, integrating spiritual values into business decision-making is a journey that demands constant vigilance, commitment, and a willingness to walk the path less traveled. It's about building a business that not only achieves success in the traditional sense but does so in a way that upholds the entrepreneur's deepest spiritual convictions. This approach fosters a business ecosystem that is not only profitable but also ethical, compassionate, and sustainable – a true reflection of the entrepreneur's spiritual ethos.

Redefining Prosperity: A Spiritual Approach to Measuring Business Success

In the dynamic arena of modern business, success is often quantified by financial achievements – soaring profits, expanding market shares, and robust financial health. However, for businesses guided by spiritual values, the definition of success transcends these traditional metrics. This perspective champions a more holistic view, intertwining spiritual fulfilment with social responsibility and sustainable growth. Measuring success through a spiritual lens involves evaluating the impact of business on various non-financial aspects such as employee satisfaction, community well-being, and environmental health. This approach fosters a comprehensive understanding of success, balancing financial stability with ethical and spiritual goals.

In the quest for a more spiritually aligned definition of success, it's crucial to recognize that business impacts numerous facets of society and the environment. Success, from a spiritual standpoint, is multidimensional, encompassing the well-being of all stakeholders, the environment, and the broader community. It's about creating value that extends beyond profit margins, contributing positively to the world.

A key component of spiritually-aligned success is the well-being of employees. A business that values its workforce, not just as employees but as individuals with their aspirations and needs, reflects a deep spiritual commitment to human dignity and respect. Employee satisfaction can be measured through regular surveys, feedback mechanisms, and workplace culture assessment. These tools offer insights into employee morale, job satisfaction, and their alignment with the company's values. Businesses with high employee satisfaction often see increased productivity, lower turnover rates, and a positive workplace environment, all indicative of holistic success.

Another crucial aspect is the business's impact on the community. Spiritually-minded businesses recognize their role as community members and strive to contribute positively to local development. This could involve community engagement programs, support for local initiatives, or partnerships with local organizations. Measuring social impact can include assessing the extent and effectiveness of community projects, community feedback, and the overall health and well-being of the community. For example, a company may measure its success by the impact of its educational programs in improving local literacy rates or by its contributions to local economic growth.

Environmental stewardship is a core tenet of many spiritual philosophies. This translates into adopting sustainable practices and minimizing environmental impact for a business. Metrics for measuring success in this area could include the reduction of carbon footprint, effective waste management, and sustainable resource use. Companies might track their progress in energy efficiency, reduction in emissions, or the percentage of recycled materials used in their products. Successful businesses in this realm comply with environmental regulations and go beyond, actively contributing to environmental conservation and sustainability.

While redefining success through a spiritual lens, financial stability remains crucial. A financially stable business is better positioned to implement ethical practices and contribute positively to employees, community, and the environment. However, financial success is not viewed as part of a broader set of values in isolation. Profitability is important but balanced with fair labour practices, ethical sourcing, and responsible marketing. A spiritually-aligned business measures success not just by what it gains, but by how these gains are achieved and utilized for the greater good.

Several businesses have successfully integrated spiritual values into their measurement of success. For instance, a technology firm might measure its success not just by its revenue but also by its advancements in ethical AI and contributions to educational initiatives. A clothing brand may define its success by shifting to sustainable fabrics, fair-trade practices, customer satisfaction, and market growth.

Many businesses struggle to balance traditional financial metrics with these broader spiritual and ethical considerations. This balance requires innovative thinking, strategic planning, and a commitment to core values. It involves a continuous process of evaluation and adaptation, ensuring that business practices not only align with spiritual values but also contribute to financial sustainability.

Measuring success through a spiritual lens invites businesses to embark on a journey of deep reflection and purposeful action. It challenges the traditional narratives of success, advocating for a more compassionate, responsible, and sustainable approach to business. By adopting this holistic view, businesses can achieve a balance of financial prosperity, social responsibility, and spiritual fulfilment, contributing to a more equitable and sustainable world. This redefined notion of success paves the way for a new era of business, where prosperity is measured in financial terms and in the positive impact on people and the planet.

Part II: Cultivating Spiritual Leadership

Ch 4. Conscious Leadership
Leading with empathy and integrity.

In the evolving leadership landscape, conscious leadership's emergence marks a significant shift from traditional models. This article delves into the foundational principles of conscious leadership, illustrating how it transcends conventional approaches by intertwining self-awareness, mindfulness, and spiritual values into the fabric of leadership. Conscious leadership is not just about decision-making and team management; it's about leading with empathy, integrity, and a holistic vision, nurturing a thriving organisation and a harmonious, value-driven community.

Understanding Conscious Leadership

Conscious leadership is a paradigm that integrates personal spiritual values with professional leadership roles. It's a holistic approach that emphasizes the well-being of all stakeholders, including employees, customers, and the broader community. Unlike traditional leadership models, which often prioritize profit and efficiency, conscious leadership focuses on creating a positive impact through ethical practices, empathetic engagement, and sustainable growth.

Core Principles of Conscious Leadership are

> **Self-Awareness: The Keystone of Conscious Leadership:** Central to conscious leadership is self-awareness. It involves understanding one's values, strengths, weaknesses, and biases. Self-aware leaders are reflective and open to feedback, constantly seeking to align their actions with their inner values. They are mindful of their decisions' influence on others and the environment.

> **Mindfulness: Leading with Presence and Thoughtfulness:** Mindfulness in leadership means being fully present in the moment aware of oneself, others, and the surrounding circumstances. It's about making decisions with a clear, focused mind, free from distractions or emotional biases. Mindful leaders are attentive to their team's needs and lead with a sense of calm and clarity.

Empathy: Connecting with the Heart: Empathy is the ability to understand and share the feelings of others. In conscious leadership, empathy translates to leading with compassion and consideration. Empathetic leaders foster a culture of trust and open communication where team members feel heard, valued, and understood.

Integrity: Leadership with Moral Courage: Integrity in leadership is about being honest, ethical, and consistent in words and actions. It involves making decisions that are not only legally right but also morally sound, even when they are not the most accessible or most profitable choices.

Sustainable and Inclusive Decision-Making: Conscious leaders make decisions that ensure long-term sustainability and inclusivity. They consider the broader impact of their decisions on society and the environment, aiming for outcomes that benefit not just the company but also the wider community.

Conscious Leadership vs. Traditional Leadership Models

Conscious leadership differs from traditional models' power, control, and success approaches. Traditional leadership often operates on hierarchical structures and emphasizes control and authority. In contrast, conscious leadership is based on collaboration, empowerment, and a shared vision. It's about leading alongside others rather than from above.

Manifestation in Daily Leadership Practices

Decision-Making with a Spiritual Lens: In conscious leadership, decision-making is guided by spiritual and ethical considerations. Leaders weigh their choices against their core values, ensuring each decision aligns with their deeper purpose.

Problem-Solving with Creativity and Compassion: Conscious leaders approach problems with creativity and compassion. They encourage innovative solutions that uphold the company's values and benefit all stakeholders.

Team Management Focused on Holistic Development: Managing a team under the conscious leadership model involves focusing on the holistic development of team members. It's about nurturing their professional skills and personal well-being, fostering an environment where everyone can thrive.

Real-world examples of conscious leadership can be seen in businesses that prioritize employee well-being, engage in fair trade, or commit to environmentally sustainable practices. Leaders in these organizations are successful in the traditional sense and revered for their ethical and compassionate leadership style.

Conscious leadership is a transformative approach that redefines the essence of being a leader. It goes beyond conventional leadership paradigms, advocating for a leadership style grounded in self-awareness, empathy, and spiritual values. By adopting this approach, leaders can create successful businesses and harmonious, value-driven communities. In an era where ethical and compassionate leadership is more critical than ever, conscious leadership stands out as the beacon for a new generation of leaders who aspire to make a meaningful difference.

Empathy in Leadership: Fostering a Connection Beyond Business

In the realm of leadership, empathy stands out as a transformative skill that transcends conventional managerial tactics. It's a quality that allows leaders to understand and share the feelings of their team, creating a bridge of connection beyond mere professional interaction. This article delves into the pivotal role of empathy in leadership, exploring how it cultivates an inclusive, supportive, and collaborative work environment. Furthermore, it provides insights into developing empathy as a skill through active listening, emotional intelligence, and compassionate communication, supplemented with practical examples and exercises.

The Power of Empathy in Leadership

Empathy, often overlooked in traditional leadership models, is a critical component in the modern leadership toolkit. It's the ability to put oneself in another's shoes to understand their feelings and perspectives. This emotional connection fosters a deeper level of trust and understanding between leaders and their teams.

Why Empathy Matters in Leadership

Building Trust and Loyalty: Empathetic leaders create a foundation of trust, encouraging open communication and a sense of security among team members. Employees who feel understood and valued are likelier to remain loyal to the leader and the organization.

Enhancing Team Collaboration: An empathetic approach to leadership fosters collaboration and cooperation within the team. Understanding the strengths and challenges of each team member enables a leader to manage group dynamics and facilitate productive teamwork effectively.

Improving Conflict Resolution: Conflicts are inevitable in any work environment. Empathy allows leaders to navigate these conflicts with sensitivity and understanding, leading to more effective and amicable resolutions.

Developing Empathy as a Leadership Skill

Empathy can be nurtured and developed as a skill, much like any other leadership competency.

Active Listening: Active listening is more than just hearing words; it's fully comprehending the speaker's message and emotions. It involves paying attention, asking clarifying questions, and refraining from judgment. This practice allows leaders to gain deeper insights into their team members' thoughts and feelings.

Emotional Intelligence: Emotional intelligence (EI) is the ability to understand and manage one's own emotions and the emotions of others. Leaders with high EI are adept at reading emotional cues and responding appropriately. Developing EI involves self-awareness, self-regulation, social awareness, and relationship management.

Compassionate Communication: Communicating with compassion involves expressing oneself honestly and empathetically, acknowledging the feelings and needs of others. This style of communication builds trust and fosters a supportive work environment.

Exercises to Enhance Empathy in Leadership

Role-Reversal Exercise: In this exercise, leaders switch roles with team members to better understand their perspectives and challenges. This can be done through role-play scenarios or by spending a day performing the duties of a team member.

Reflective Journaling: Keeping a journal to reflect on daily interactions can help leaders become more aware of their empathetic responses and identify areas for improvement.

Feedback Sessions: Regular feedback sessions, both giving and receiving, can enhance a leader's understanding of the impact of their actions and decisions on others.

Empathy in Action: Real-Life Examples

Empathy in leadership is not just theoretical; it has practical applications with tangible benefits. For example, a team leader who actively listens to concerns about workload and deadlines and responds by adjusting project timelines demonstrates empathy in action. Similarly, a manager who acknowledges and supports an employee going through personal challenges fosters a culture of empathy.

Challenges in Practising Empathy

While empathy is a valuable skill, practising it can sometimes be challenging. Leaders might struggle with balancing empathy with maintaining authority or making tough decisions. Overcoming these challenges involves recognizing that empathy does not equate to leniency or avoidance of difficult choices but is a way of executing these decisions with understanding and respect.

Empathy in leadership is about more than just effective management; it's about connecting with people at a human level. By developing and practising empathetic leadership, leaders can create productive work environments, nurturing, and fulfilling. Empathetic leadership brings a human touch to the workplace, encouraging loyalty, collaboration, and a shared sense of purpose. As businesses evolve, leaders who harness the power of empathy are well-equipped to lead their teams towards success, both in business and in building meaningful workplace relationships.

Integrity: The Bedrock of Spiritual Leadership

In leadership, integrity stands as a beacon, guiding leaders through the complexities of modern business landscapes. Particularly in spiritual leadership, integrity – defined as steadfast adherence to a strict moral or ethical code – becomes not just an attribute but the cornerstone. This article delves into the crucial role of integrity in conscious leadership, examining how it aligns leadership practices with spiritual values. It also discusses the challenges leaders face in maintaining integrity and its profound impact on building trust, credibility, and a positive organizational reputation.

The Essence of Integrity in Leadership

Integrity in leadership transcends the simple act of doing the right thing. It's a commitment to consistently live by one's values and principles, regardless of the situation. In the context of spiritual leadership, this means aligning one's actions with deeply held spiritual and moral convictions. It's about making decisions that drive business success and resonate with the leader's inner moral compass.

Why Integrity Matters

Integrity is fundamental in building trust. When leaders act consistently and ethically, they earn the trust of their employees, customers, and stakeholders. This trust is the foundation of solid relationships, essential for any successful organization.

A leader's credibility is closely tied to their integrity. Leaders known for their integrity are often respected within their industries and beyond. This reputation for integrity becomes a powerful asset for both the leader and the organization.

For leaders espousing spiritual values, integrity acts as a moral guiding light. It ensures that their decisions and actions are profitable, ethically sound, and spiritually aligned.

Challenges to Maintaining Integrity

Maintaining integrity can be challenging in the fast-paced and often high-pressure business world. Leaders frequently face situations where the right choice isn't the easiest one.

> Leaders may encounter situations where they have to choose between competing interests, where the ethically correct decision may conflict with business interests.

> Market pressures, competition, and financial targets can sometimes tempt leaders to cut corners or compromise on their values.

> Leaders often navigate complex interpersonal dynamics where maintaining integrity can mean making tough decisions that may not please everyone.

Maintaining Integrity in Difficult Situations

Maintaining integrity, especially in challenging situations, requires a strong sense of self and a clear understanding of one's values.

1. **Clear Ethical Standards:**

   - Leaders should establish and adhere to clear ethical standards. These standards should guide all business practices and decisions.

2. **Open Communication:**

   - Transparency and open communication are vital. Leaders should clearly communicate their values and ethical standards to their teams and stakeholders.

3. **Accountability:**

   - Leaders should hold themselves and their teams accountable for maintaining ethical standards. This might involve regular ethical training and creating systems for reporting and addressing unethical behaviour.

The Impact of Integrity on Leadership

The impact of integrity in leadership is far-reaching. Organizations led by people of integrity often enjoy long-term success. Ethical business practices build lasting customer relationships and create a positive brand image. Integrity in leadership contributes to a positive workplace culture, boosting employee morale and engagement. Employees are more likely to be committed and motivated when they respect their leaders' values. Leaders with integrity leave a lasting legacy. They are remembered not just for their business achievements but for the positive impact they had on their organizations and communities.

Real-Life Examples of Integrity in Leadership

Many successful leaders exemplify integrity in their actions. For instance, a CEO who prioritizes fair labour practices over cheaper but unethical alternatives demonstrates integrity. Another example is a leader who transparently communicates a company's challenges and the steps being taken to address them, maintaining honesty with stakeholders.

Integrity in spiritual leadership is not a mere buzzword; it's a way of being. It's about aligning every decision and action with moral and spiritual beliefs. Leaders who uphold integrity navigate the business world with a moral compass that guides them to professional success, personal fulfilment, and a more profound sense of purpose. In a world often dominated by short-term gains and flexible morals, integrity is the bedrock of authentic, spiritually-aligned leadership.

Ch 5. Building a Soulful Team Hiring and team dynamics in a spiritually-aligned business

In the heart of every spiritually-aligned business lies a soulful team, a collective that resonates not just with skills and expertise but with the core spiritual values of the organization. Chapter 5, "Building a Soulful Team: Hiring and Team Dynamics in a Spiritually-Aligned Business," explores the art and science of cultivating a team that embodies the ethos of spiritual alignment. This chapter is a guide, a compass of sorts, for entrepreneurs who seek to infuse their spiritual values into every aspect of their team-building process, from hiring to nurturing a harmonious team dynamic.

Creating a soulful team transcends the conventional approach to hiring and team management. It involves attracting and retaining individuals who excel in their professional roles and deeply connect with the spiritual mission of the business. This chapter will unveil the importance of aligning not just the skills and experiences of team members with business needs, but also aligning their values and beliefs with the spiritual heartbeat of the organization.

The journey begins with the hiring process, the first step in building a team that shares the business's spiritual values. This segment of the chapter delves into how to identify candidates whose personal values resonate with those of the company. It includes insights on tailoring job descriptions to attract suitable candidates, innovative interviewing techniques to assess spiritual and ethical alignment, and evaluating potential team members for a fit beyond the resume.

Once the right individuals are on board, the focus shifts to nurturing a team culture that breathes the spiritual values of the business. This section discusses how to onboard new members in a way that immerses them in the company's spiritual ethos. It emphasizes creating a work environment where spiritual values are lived and experienced daily, fostering a sense of community, empathy, and shared purpose.

In any team, dynamics can be complex and evolving. This chapter will guide you through managing these dynamics in a manner that upholds and reflects the spiritual values of the business. It explores practical ways to handle conflicts, encourage collaborative problem-solving, and foster open communication, all grounded in the spiritual principles that underpin the industry. This part of the chapter is crucial for leaders seeking to maintain harmony and productivity within their teams while staying true to their spiritual mission.

As businesses grow and evolve, maintaining the spiritual integrity of a team can become challenging. This section offers strategies for keeping the team aligned with the core spiritual values of the business, even amidst significant changes or growth phases. It's about ensuring the spiritual ethos remains at the forefront of all team development and business evolution strategies.

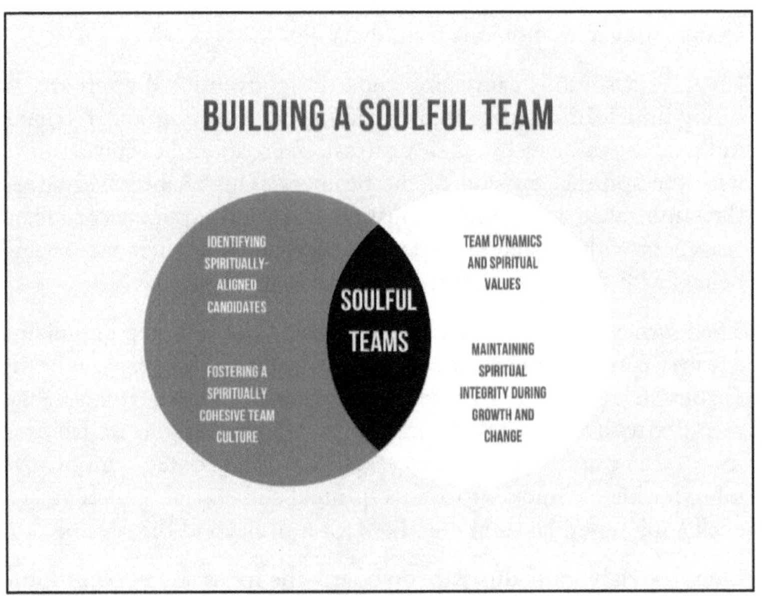

In essence, "Building a Soulful Team" is not just about assembling a group of individuals to carry out business functions; it's about creating a microcosm of the business's spiritual ethos. It's about fostering a work environment where team members feel valued for their professional contributions and their spiritual and ethical alignment with the business. This chapter aims to equip spiritually-minded entrepreneurs with the knowledge, tools, and inspiration to build teams that are effective in their roles and deeply connected to their business's spiritual mission, creating a harmonious and purpose-driven work environment.

Harmonizing Spirit and Skill: Identifying Ideal Candidates for Spiritually-Aligned Businesses

In the journey of creating a soulful and spiritually-aligned business, one of the most crucial steps is building a team that not only possesses the necessary skills and experience but also shares in the spiritual ethos of the organization. This alignment is essential for fostering a harmonious and effective work environment. This article delves into the strategies for identifying such candidates, techniques for crafting compelling job descriptions, and methods for assessing spiritual and ethical compatibility during the interview process.

The Importance of Spiritual Alignment in Team Building

A team that resonates with the spiritual values of a business is instrumental in creating an environment where these values are lived and breathed. Such alignment leads to enhanced teamwork, a shared sense of purpose, and a more profound commitment to the organization's mission.

Crafting Job Descriptions to Attract the Right Candidates

Reflecting Core Values: The first step in attracting spiritually-aligned candidates is to ensure that the job description reflects the business's core values. This involves more than listing job responsibilities and qualifications; it requires infusing the spiritual essence of the business into the description.

Clear Communication of Spiritual Ethos: The job description should clearly communicate the spiritual ethos of the business, outlining how these values translate into everyday operations and expectations.

Highlighting the Spiritual Journey: Prospective candidates should be able to discern what the job entails and the spiritual journey they would be part of. This can be achieved by incorporating testimonials or stories from current employees about their experiences working in a spiritually-aligned environment.

The Interview Process: Gauging Value Alignment

The interview process is critical in assessing a candidate's alignment with the business's spiritual values.

Asking the Right Questions: Questions should be designed to elicit responses that reveal a candidate's value system. For example, it can be insightful to ask about a time when they had to make a difficult ethical decision or how they see their personal values aligning with the company's values.

Behavioral Interviews: Behavioral interviewing techniques can be particularly effective. By asking candidates to describe past experiences and how they handled specific situations, interviewers can gauge how their actions and decisions align with the spiritual values of the business.

Assessing Emotional and Spiritual Intelligence: Emotional and spiritual intelligence are crucial for a spiritually-aligned business. Assessing a candidate's ability to empathize and connect with others on a deeper level and understand their spiritual journey can be as important as their technical skills.

Methods for Assessing Spiritual and Ethical Compatibility

Personality and Values Assessments: Utilizing personality and values assessments can provide additional insights into a candidate's alignment with the business's spiritual ethos.

Reference Checks: Conducting thorough reference checks where past behaviors and attitudes can be discussed can also help in assessing a candidate's spiritual and ethical compatibility.

Examples of Spiritually-Aligned Hiring

A Wellness Company: A wellness company, for example, might look for candidates who have experience in health and fitness, practice mindfulness, and have a deep commitment to holistic well-being. During interviews, they might ask candidates to share how they incorporate wellness and mindfulness into their daily lives.

An Eco-Friendly Business: An eco-friendly business might seek candidates passionate about environmental conservation. They could include a question in their interview process about the candidate's involvement in environmental initiatives or how they practice sustainability in their personal life.

The Long-Term Benefits of Spiritually-Aligned Hiring

Hiring candidates aligned with the business's spiritual values has long-term benefits. It leads to higher employee satisfaction, lower turnover rates, and a more cohesive team dynamic. Employees who share the same spiritual values as the business are more likely to be engaged, motivated, and committed to the company's vision.

Identifying and hiring candidates who resonate with the spiritual values of a business is a nuanced process that goes beyond assessing skills and experience. It involves crafting job descriptions that reflect the spiritual ethos of the company, asking the right questions during interviews, and employing various methods to assess a candidate's spiritual and ethical compatibility. By ensuring that new hires are aligned with the spiritual values of the business, leaders can build teams that are skilled and, effective and deeply connected to the business's broader mission, fostering a productive and spiritually fulfilling workplace.

Cultivating Unity: Establishing a Spiritually Cohesive Team Culture

In the intricate business world, cultivating a team culture that resonates with a company's spiritual values is beneficial and essential for long-term success and employee satisfaction. This article delves into the various strategies and practices involved in fostering a team culture that reflects a business's spiritual values. From onboarding new team members, integrating spiritual values into daily work interactions, and creating a supportive, empathetic, and respectful workplace, each aspect plays a crucial role in building a spiritually cohesive team. Additionally, the article emphasizes the importance of inclusivity and respect for diverse spiritual beliefs, ensuring a harmonious and productive work environment.

The Foundation of a Spiritually Cohesive Team Culture

Building a team culture that aligns with the spiritual values of a business begins with a clear understanding of what those values are and how they translate into the everyday workings of the team. It involves a deliberate effort to weave these values into the fabric of the company's culture, making them an intrinsic part of the team's identity.

Onboarding with a Spiritual Focus

Introducing New Members to the Company's Values: The onboarding process is critical to introduce new team members to the company's spiritual values. This can be achieved through workshops, team-building activities, and discussions that highlight the importance of these values in the company's mission and operations.

Mentorship Programs: Pairing new employees with mentors who exemplify the company's spiritual values can provide them with guidance and a deeper understanding of how these values are embodied within the company.

Incorporating Values into Training Materials: Training materials and company handbooks should include sections that explain the spiritual values of the company, providing concrete examples of how these values are implemented in day-to-day operations.

Integrating Spiritual Values into Everyday Work Interactions

Regular Reflection and Discussion: Encourage regular team meetings or discussions focused on the company's spiritual values. These discussions can revolve around how these values have been or can be implemented in ongoing projects or daily tasks.

Recognition and Reinforcement: Recognize and reinforce behaviors and actions that reflect the company's spiritual values. This can be done through acknowledgement in team meetings, performance reviews, or through a formal recognition program.

Creating a Supportive, Empathetic, and Respectful Workplace

Fostering Open Communication: Encourage open communication and create safe spaces where team members can express their thoughts and feelings without fear of judgment. This fosters an environment of mutual respect and understanding.

Team Building Activities: Organize team-building activities that are aligned with the company's spiritual values. These activities can range from community service projects to mindfulness and wellness workshops.

Conflict Resolution with a Spiritual Approach: Adopt conflict resolution strategies that are in line with the company's spiritual values. This could involve mediation techniques that emphasize understanding, empathy, and finding mutually beneficial solutions.

Inclusivity and Respect for Diverse Spiritual Beliefs

Celebrating Diversity: Celebrate the diverse spiritual beliefs within the team. This can involve hosting cultural awareness days or discussion groups where team members can share and learn about different spiritual traditions.

Inclusive Policies: Implement inclusive policies that respect various spiritual practices. This might include flexible schedules to accommodate religious observances or creating spaces for prayer or meditation.

Examples of Spiritually Cohesive Team Cultures

A Tech Company Focused on Mindfulness: A tech company might integrate mindfulness practices into their daily routines, offering meditation sessions and training on mindful communication to enhance focus and reduce stress.

A Retail Business with a Commitment to Compassion: A retail business could establish a culture of compassion by engaging in community service, encouraging employees to volunteer, and implementing fair and ethical treatment of customers and employees.

Fostering a spiritually cohesive team culture is a journey that requires continuous effort and dedication. It's about creating an environment where the spiritual values of the business are not just words on a wall but living principles that guide and shape the team's interactions and decisions. Such a culture not only enhances team harmony and productivity but also contributes to each team member's personal growth and fulfilment, ultimately leading to a more purposeful and impactful business.

Spiritual Synergy: Nurturing Team Dynamics through Shared Values

In today's diverse and dynamic work environments, team dynamics are crucial in determining the success and harmony within organizations. More than ever, there's a growing recognition of the profound impact spiritual values can have on these dynamics. This article delves into understanding how spiritual values can shape team interactions, enhance collaboration, and address conflicts. It explores various methods and strategies to embed these values into the core of team dynamics, fostering an atmosphere of open communication, mutual respect, and collective problem-solving.

The Influence of Spiritual Values on Team Dynamics

Spiritual values, when integrated into team dynamics, can transform mere groups of individuals into cohesive units bound by a shared sense of purpose and understanding. These values often encompass empathy, integrity, respect, and compassion. When teams operate from this value-driven perspective, they navigate work challenges more effectively and collaboratively.

Harmonizing Conflicts with Spiritual Principles

Conflicts are inevitable in any team setting. However, addressing these conflicts through the lens of spiritual values can lead to more empathetic and constructive resolutions.

> **Empathetic Listening and Understanding:** Encouraging team members to practice compassionate listening can significantly de-escalate conflicts. This involves understanding the perspectives and emotions behind each team member's viewpoint rather than just the content of their arguments.

Principled Conflict Resolution: Adopting conflict resolution methods that align with spiritual values is key. This could involve mediation techniques focusing on finding common ground and solutions aligning with the team's shared values.

Post-Conflict Reflection: After resolving conflicts, it's beneficial to have a reflection session. This helps in understanding the root causes of conflicts and how spiritual values can be better applied to prevent similar issues in the future.

Encouraging Open and Honest Communication

Open and honest communication is the bedrock of effective team dynamics. Integrating spiritual values into communication strategies can enhance this openness.

Regular Check-ins and Feedback Sessions: Scheduling regular check-ins and feedback sessions where team members can share their thoughts and feelings fosters a culture of openness.

Non-Violent Communication Training: Training in non-violent communication can help team members express themselves in honest yet respectful ways, reducing the likelihood of misunderstandings and conflicts.

Collective Problem-Solving with a Spiritual Touch

Collective problem-solving incorporating spiritual values can lead to more innovative and inclusive solutions.

Value-Based Brainstorming Sessions: Organizing brainstorming sessions that start with a reminder of the team's core spiritual values can set the tone for a collaborative and respectful problem-solving process.

Inclusive Decision-Making: Ensuring that all team members have a voice in decision-making and that decisions align with the team's spiritual values enhances the sense of ownership and commitment to the solutions.

Enhancing Collaboration, Creativity, and Respect

When team members share spiritual values, they tend to collaborate more effectively, respecting each other's ideas and contributions.

Team Building Activities Focused on Values: Conducting team-building activities that emphasize the team's spiritual values can strengthen bonds and enhance mutual respect.

Creative Projects with a Value Focus: Encouraging creative projects that align with or express the team's spiritual values can inspire innovation and a shared purpose.

Examples of Value-Driven Team Dynamics

A Healthcare Team Embracing Compassion: A team in a healthcare setting might integrate compassion into their daily interactions, ensuring that this core value guides every patient interaction.

An IT Team Focused on Integrity: An IT team could prioritize integrity in their work, ensuring that all projects are handled with honesty and transparency fostering trust within the team and with clients.

Incorporating spiritual values into team dynamics is not a one-time task but a continuous journey. It requires commitment, practice, and a willingness to adapt and grow together as a team. By embracing spiritual values, teams can transcend traditional work relationships, creating environments that are not only productive but also nurturing and fulfilling. In these spaces, challenges are met with empathy, creativity flourishes within the framework of mutual respect, and success is measured by outcomes and the quality of interactions and relationships built along the way.

Steadfast Spirit: Upholding Spiritual Integrity Amidst Growth and Change

In the evolving journey of a business, growth and change are inevitable. However, during these phases, one of the most profound challenges spiritually-aligned companies faces is maintaining the team's spiritual integrity. As a business scales up, navigates market shifts, or encounters internal challenges, new pressures and priorities can overshadow the core spiritual values that once defined its operations. This article delves into strategies for preserving a team's spiritual essence during these crucial periods, ensuring that the spiritual ethos continues to guide all aspects of team development and business evolution.

Spiritual integrity in business is about aligning every decision, strategy, and interaction with the core spiritual values of the organization. It forms the moral compass that guides a company through the complexities of the commercial world. As a business grows or faces changes, this compass becomes even more crucial, serving as an anchor that maintains the business's unique identity and purpose.

Challenges in Sustaining Spiritual Integrity During Growth and Change

Dilution of Core Values: Rapid growth or significant changes can sometimes dilute the business's core spiritual values as the focus shifts towards new goals, markets, or operational challenges.

Pressure to Conform: Market pressures and the need to stay competitive can sometimes lead teams to adopt practices that conflict with their spiritual principles.

Internal Conflicts: Changes within the team, leadership, or strategy can lead to internal conflicts, challenging the team's ability to stay aligned with their spiritual values.

Strategies for Maintaining Spiritual Integrity

Clear Articulation of Spiritual Values: Continually articulate and reinforce the spiritual values that define the business. This can be done through regular team meetings, training sessions, and communication strategies that keep these values at everyone's mind.

Incorporating Values in Decision-Making: Ensure that all business decisions, big or small, are made with the spiritual values in mind. This requires conscious consideration of how each decision aligns with these values.

Leadership as Custodians of Spiritual Integrity: Leadership plays a critical role in upholding spiritual integrity. Leaders must embody spiritual values and consistently demonstrate their commitment to these principles.

Strategies for Team Alignment During Growth and Change

Regular Spiritual Retreats and Workshops: Organizing retreats or workshops focused on the business's spiritual values can help realign the team, especially during significant change or growth periods.

Spiritual Mentoring and Support: Mentoring and supporting team members to help them navigate changes while staying true to the spiritual ethos can be beneficial.

Transparent Communication: Maintain open and honest communication channels where team members can express their concerns or suggestions regarding maintaining spiritual integrity.

Adapting to Market Changes Without Losing Spiritual Focus

Innovative Approaches Aligned with Spiritual Values: Explore innovative business strategies and solutions that align with spiritual values, even when adapting to market changes.

Balancing Commercial and Spiritual Goals: Find a balance between commercial objectives and spiritual values, ensuring that one does not overshadow the other.

Staying True to the Ethos in Marketing and Operations: Ensure that marketing strategies and operational changes remain faithful to the spiritual ethos of the business.

Examples of Spiritual Integrity in Action

A Socially Conscious Business: For instance, a socially conscious business facing market pressure to outsource cheaply may choose to continue employing local artisans, aligning with its values of community support and fair labour practices.

An Environmentally-Focused Company: An environmentally-focused company might turn down lucrative opportunities that contradict its sustainability commitment, instead seeking partnerships and projects that align with its environmental ethos.

Maintaining spiritual integrity during growth, change, or crisis is about staying true to the foundational principles that define a business's identity. It involves a consistent, conscious effort to ensure that every aspect of the company, from its operations to its interactions, reflects its spiritual values. By doing so, companies preserve their unique character and purpose and foster a more profound sense of meaning and fulfilment among their team members. In a world where the bottom line often drives companies, those who uphold their spiritual integrity stand out, creating a legacy that goes beyond financial success and resonates on a deeper, more personal level with their teams, customers, and the wider community.

Ch 6. Mindful Communication
Fostering openness and understanding in the workplace

In the bustling corridors of modern workplaces, where diverse ideas, personalities, and goals converge, communication forms the vital bridge that connects individuals and teams. However, the essence of proper communication often gets lost in the pursuit of efficiency and productivity. This chapter opens a window to a different approach, one that is rooted deeply in spiritual principles and mindfulness. This chapter is a journey into understanding and implementing mindful communication, a tool for effective interaction and fostering a workplace environment rich in empathy, clarity, and mutual respect.

As we navigate the complexities of professional interactions, mindful communication stands out as a beacon, guiding us towards more meaningful and profound connections. At its core, conscious communication is about being present, aware, and empathetic. It transcends the mechanical exchange of information and delves into creating an atmosphere of openness and understanding.

This chapter begins by exploring mindful communication and why it is especially crucial in today's fast-paced business environment. It reveals how mindful communication goes beyond just the spoken word; it encompasses active listening, understanding non-verbal cues, and responding with thoughtfulness and consideration.

We delve deeper into the art of active listening, an essential skill in mindful communication. Active listening involves fully concentrating on what is being said rather than passively hearing the speaker's message. This section outlines techniques and exercises to develop and enhance active listening skills, fostering a culture of proper understanding and empathy within the workplace.

One of the most vital aspects of mindful communication is how it equips us to handle difficult conversations and conflicts. This chapter provides practical guidance on applying mindfulness in challenging interactions, ensuring that communication remains respectful, clear, and compassionate even in the face of disagreement or tension.

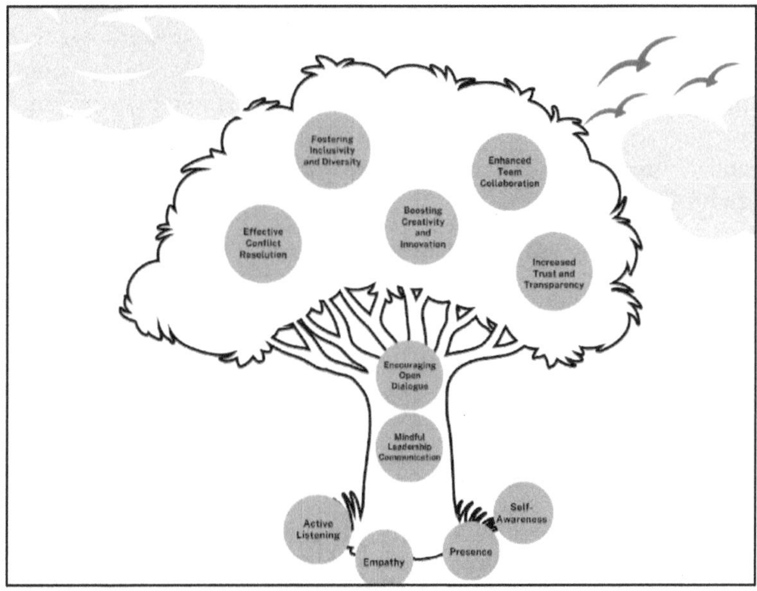

The role of mindful communication in leadership is also a focus of this chapter. It emphasizes how leaders can use mindful communication to build trust, encourage openness, and create an inclusive team environment. Through examples and case studies, we explore how leaders can model aware communication practices and set a tone that promotes understanding and collaboration.

Finally, the chapter addresses how to embed mindful communication practices into the organisation's very fabric. From structured training programs to informal daily practices, we explore various strategies to foster an environment where mindful communication is the norm, not the exception.

Mindful Communication: The Heartbeat of a Spiritually-Aligned Workplace

In the tapestry of today's professional landscape, communication forms the thread that weaves the fabric of workplace interactions. However, when imbued with mindfulness and spiritual awareness, communication transcends its ordinary boundaries, becoming a potent tool for nurturing understanding, empathy, and connectivity. This article explores the essence of mindful communication within a spiritual context, focusing on how it encompasses much more than the exchange of words – it is about listening deeply, understanding profoundly, and responding with awareness and compassion. Here, we unravel how mindful communication aligns with spiritual values and fosters a harmonious, respectful, and honest workplace environment.

Understanding Mindful Communication

Mindful communication is an approach that integrates mindfulness - the practice of being present and fully engaged with whatever we're doing at the moment - into how we interact with others. It's about being consciously present in our conversations, whether speaking or listening.

Components of Mindful Communication

1. **Active Listening:** More than just hearing words, active listening involves fully concentrating on the speaker, understanding their message, and responding thoughtfully. It's about listening with the intent to understand, not just to reply.

2. **Empathy:** Empathy in communication is about genuinely understanding and sharing another person's feelings. It involves putting ourselves in their shoes and viewing things from their perspective.

3. **Awareness and Presence:** This involves being fully present in the conversation, free from distractions. It's about giving the speaker our undivided attention and engaging with their words sincerely.

Aligning with Spiritual Values

Mindful communication is deeply aligned with spiritual values, fostering an environment of mutual respect, understanding, and honesty.

Empathy and Compassion: By actively listening and empathizing, we acknowledge the speaker's feelings and perspectives, fostering a sense of compassion and connection.

Honesty and Integrity: Mindful communication encourages honesty and integrity, ensuring that the information shared is truthful and transparent.

Respect and Understanding: This approach to communication inherently respects the speaker, values their input, and seeks to understand their viewpoint.

The Role of Mindful Communication in Conflict Resolution

In resolving conflicts, mindful communication plays a pivotal role. By listening actively and empathetically, misunderstandings can be clarified, and solutions that satisfy all parties can be found. Mindful communication ensures that conflicts are handled in a way that maintains respect and understanding, even amidst disagreements.

Implementing Mindful Communication in the Workplace

Training and Workshops: Conducting regular training sessions and workshops on mindful communication can equip team members with the necessary skills and awareness.

Mindfulness Practices: Encouraging mindfulness practices like meditation can enhance an individual's presence and awareness during conversations.

Creating a Culture of Openness: Establishing a workplace culture that values open, honest, and empathetic communication sets the foundation for mindful interactions.

Some Examples of Mindful Communication in Action are

Team Meetings: During team meetings, each member is given the floor to speak without interruption, ensuring their ideas and concerns are heard and understood.

Feedback Sessions: In feedback sessions, both parties actively listen, expressing their views honestly while maintaining empathy and understanding.

Overcoming Challenges in Mindful Communication

Implementing mindful communication in a workplace can be challenging, especially in high-pressure environments. However, these challenges can be navigated successfully with consistent practice and a commitment to upholding spiritual values.

Mindful communication, imbued with spiritual values, is not just a skill but a way of being. It transforms the workplace into a space where every interaction is an opportunity for deeper connection, understanding, and growth. By embracing this approach, organizations can foster a culture that is effective in achieving its goals and nourishes the spirit and soul of every individual involved. In a world where disconnect and miscommunication are rampant, mindful communication is a beacon of hope, guiding us towards more compassionate, respectful, and meaningful interactions.

Harmonizing Hearts and Minds: Mastering Active Listening and Empathetic Engagement

Active listening and empathetic engagement play pivotal roles in the intricate dance of communication, transforming ordinary conversations into deep, meaningful exchanges. The spiritual workplace, striving for a higher level of connection and understanding, mainly benefits from these skills. This article explores the profound impact of active listening and empathetic engagement as core components of mindful communication. It delves into practical strategies for honing these skills, including techniques like paraphrasing, reflecting, and understanding non-verbal cues, and discusses how they foster an environment of mutual respect and trust, pillars of a spiritually nurturing workplace.

The Art of Active Listening

Active listening is more than just hearing words; it's a dynamic process of understanding, interpreting, and responding to communication thoughtfully. It's about fully immersing oneself in the conversation, not only with the ears but with the heart and mind.

Key Components of Active Listening

> **Full Attention:** This involves focusing entirely on the speaker, putting aside distractions, and refraining from formulating responses while they are still speaking.

> **Non-Verbal Cues:** Non-verbal communication such as nodding, eye contact, and appropriate facial expressions, can significantly demonstrate attention and understanding.

Avoiding Interrupting: Allowing the speaker to finish their thoughts without interruption is crucial for active listening.

Techniques to Enhance Active Listening

Paraphrasing: Repeating what was said in your own words is a powerful way to show that you have understood the message. It helps in clarifying and confirming the speaker's intent.

Reflecting is about acknowledging the feelings and emotions behind the speaker's words. It involves making statements like, "It sounds like you felt really disappointed when..."

Asking Open-Ended Questions: Questions that cannot be answered with a simple 'yes' or 'no' encourage elaboration and provide deeper insights into the speaker's thoughts and feelings.

Empathetic Engagement: The Heart of Spiritual Communication

Empathy in communication is about connecting with the speaker on an emotional level. It's about understanding their feelings and perspectives, whether or not you agree with them.

Understanding vs. Agreeing: Empathetic engagement does not necessarily mean agreement with the speaker's point of view but rather understanding it from their perspective.

Validating Feelings: Acknowledging and validating the speaker's feelings, regardless of your personal opinions, is a critical aspect of empathetic engagement.

The Impact of Active Listening and Empathetic Engagement in the Workplace

Building Trust and Respect: These skills foster an environment where team members feel valued and understood, leading to stronger trust and respect among colleagues.

Enhancing Team Collaboration: When team members practice active listening and empathetic engagement, it leads to more effective collaboration, as everyone feels their contributions are being acknowledged and valued.

Conflict Resolution: In conflict situations, these skills can de-escalate tensions and lead to more constructive resolutions.

Implementing Active Listening and Empathetic Engagement in Daily Interactions

Regular Training and Workshops: Training sessions focused on active listening and empathetic communication can help team members develop and refine these skills.

Mindfulness Practices: Encouraging mindfulness practices like meditation can enhance one's listening ability and engagement empathetically.

Role-Playing Exercises: Role-playing exercises can provide practical experience and insights into applying these skills in real-life scenarios.

Examples of Active Listening and Empathetic Engagement

A Manager Addressing Team Concerns: A manager actively listens to a team member's concerns about workload, paraphrases their points for clarity, and acknowledges the stress they are feeling, leading to a discussion on solutions.

A Customer Service Interaction: A customer service representative listens empathetically to a customer's complaint, validates their frustration, and works towards a resolution, thereby turning a potentially negative experience into a positive one.

Active listening and empathetic engagement are not mere tools for efficient communication but heartbeats of a spiritually nurturing work environment. By mastering these skills, individuals and teams can create a workspace that resonates with understanding, compassion, and genuine connection. In the grand symphony of workplace interactions, these skills harmonize the hearts and minds of all, fostering a culture where spiritual values and human connections flourish.

Mindfulness during Storms: Guiding Difficult Conversations with Compassion

Navigating difficult conversations is an inevitable aspect of both personal and professional life. However, when these conversations are approached with mindfulness and a deep adherence to spiritual values, they can transform from potential conflicts into opportunities for growth and understanding. This article delves into the art of applying mindful communication principles during challenging discussions, focusing on managing conflicts, delivering constructive feedback, and handling emotionally charged conversations. It provides practical guidance on remaining anchored in spiritual values throughout these interactions and using mindful communication to foster positive, compassionate outcomes that honor the dignity and perspectives of all parties involved.

The Role of Mindfulness in Difficult Conversations

Mindfulness, the practice of being fully present and engaged in the moment without judgment, is a powerful tool in navigating tough discussions. It allows us to approach conversations with a clear, calm mind and a compassionate heart, essential for resolving conflicts constructively.

Key Aspects of Mindful Communication in Challenging Situations

Presence and Awareness: Staying fully present, focused on the conversation at hand, and aware of both your own reactions and the other person's responses.

Non-reactivity: Practising non-reactivity involves acknowledging your emotions without letting them overpower the conversation or dictate your responses.

Empathetic Listening: Active and empathetic listening helps understand the other person's perspective, even if it differs from yours.

Managing Conflicts with a Mindful Approach

Conflicts, when addressed mindfully, can lead to deeper understanding and resolution.

Recognizing Emotional Triggers: Identifying personal emotional triggers helps manage your conflict responses.

Maintaining Calm and Composure: Keeping a calm demeanour, even in the face of provocation, sets a constructive tone for the conversation.

Seeking Common Ground: Focusing on finding common ground or mutual interests as a basis for resolution.

Delivering Constructive Feedback Mindfully

Providing feedback is an art, especially when it involves criticism or negative observations.

The Sandwich Approach: This involves starting with a positive comment, followed by constructive feedback, and concluding with a positive note or a suggestion for improvement.

Clarity and Specificity: Being clear and specific about the issues helps prevent misunderstandings and defensiveness.

Focusing on Behaviors, Not Personalities: Addressing specific behaviours or actions rather than making personal judgments or accusations.

Handling Emotional Conversations with Compassion

Emotionally charged conversations require an extra level of sensitivity and understanding.

Acknowledging Emotions: Recognizing and validating the emotions involved, yours and the other person's, without judgment.

Using "I" Statements: Expressing your feelings and perspectives using "I" statements to avoid blame and defensiveness.

Allowing Space for Expression: Giving the other person space to express their emotions and perspective fully.

Staying Grounded in Spiritual Values

It's essential to remain grounded in your spiritual values throughout difficult conversations.

Reflecting on Core Values: Reminding yourself of your core spiritual values, such as empathy, respect, and honesty, can guide your responses and interactions.

Practising Patience and Tolerance: Even in challenging situations, demonstrating patience and tolerance reflects a deep commitment to your spiritual principles.

Seeking the Higher Good: Focusing on the higher good or the larger purpose of the conversation can help approach it with a positive and constructive mindset.

Examples of Mindful Communication in Difficult Conversations

A Workplace Disagreement: In a scenario where two team members disagree on a project approach, using mindful communication involves each party actively listening to the other's viewpoint, acknowledging their concerns, and collaboratively finding a solution that respects both perspectives.

Delivering Performance Feedback: When a manager needs to address an employee's performance issues, approaching the conversation with clarity, empathy, and specific suggestions for improvement while maintaining respect for the employee's efforts and dignity exemplifies mindful communication.

Difficult conversations can become gateways to greater understanding, stronger relationships, and personal and professional growth when navigated with mindfulness and spiritual integrity. By embracing the principles of mindful communication, individuals and teams can turn potential conflicts into opportunities for constructive change, ensuring that every interaction, no matter how challenging, is approached with compassion, respect, and a commitment to positive outcomes.

Part III: Strategies for Spiritual and Business Growth

Ch 7. Innovative Thinking with a Spiritual Lens: Encouraging creativity and spiritual insight

In a world where business and spirituality are often viewed as separate realms, combining innovative thinking with a spiritual lens presents a refreshing and transformative perspective. Chapter 7, "Innovative Thinking with a Spiritual Lens: Encouraging Creativity and Spiritual Insight," invites readers into a unique exploration of how spiritual values and principles can not only coexist with but actively enhance business innovation. This chapter unveils the synergy between spirituality and creativity, illustrating how a spiritual approach to innovation can lead to profound insights, sustainable growth, and a deeper sense of purpose in business.

As we embark on this journey, we confront the misconception that spirituality and business operate in silos. Instead, we discover that spiritual principles such as mindfulness, interconnectedness, and empathy are potent catalysts for creative thought and innovative problem-solving. Intertwining these realms opens up new business horizons, fostering environments where innovation is not just about economic success but also about nurturing the human spirit and contributing positively to the world.

This chapter begins by exploring how spiritual values can act as a catalyst for innovation. It delves into the ways spiritual practices and principles can stimulate creative thinking, inspire new ideas, and lead to innovative solutions that are both effective and ethically sound. Through real-life examples and case studies, we illustrate how businesses that embrace spirituality often find themselves at the forefront of innovation, driven by a deeper understanding of their purpose and a commitment to making a positive impact.

The focus then shifts to how businesses can create a culture that encourages creativity and spiritual growth. This includes practical strategies for nurturing an environment where team members feel valued for their professional skills, holistic well-being, and spiritual insights. We explore how such a culture can lead to a more engaged, motivated, and innovative workforce capable of thinking outside the box and pushing the boundaries of conventional business practices.

An integral part of this chapter is the exploration of mindfulness practices and their role in enhancing creativity. We discuss how techniques like meditation, reflective practices, and presence can open the mind to unexplored possibilities and new ways of thinking. This section provides readers with practical tools and exercises to integrate mindfulness into their daily routines, fostering mental clarity and openness essential for innovative thinking.

Finally, the chapter addresses the challenge of maintaining spiritual integrity in pursuing competitive innovation. It offers insights on how businesses can navigate this delicate balance, ensuring their innovative endeavours align with their spiritual values and principles. This section underscores the importance of ethical considerations in innovation, the role of authenticity and integrity, and the transformative potential of purpose-driven innovation.

"Innovative Thinking with a Spiritual Lens: Encouraging Creativity and Spiritual Insight" is not just a chapter; it's an invitation to reimagine the role of spirituality in the business world. It encourages readers to see innovation as a tool for economic success and an opportunity for spiritual growth and positive global impact. As we turn each page, we uncover the profound and harmonious relationship between spirituality and innovation, revealing how they can lead to a more fulfilling, responsible, and visionary approach to business.

The Harmonious Blend: Spirituality and Innovation in Business

In modern business, the fusion of spirituality and innovation emerges as a potent and transformative force. This confluence represents a paradigm shift, where the pursuit of innovative solutions is not only driven by profit but also guided by deeper spiritual values like mindfulness, empathy, and interconnectedness. The article delves into how spiritual principles can inspire and revitalize innovative thinking in the business realm, leading to ethically resonant and creatively vibrant growth. Through this exploration, we uncover examples of businesses that have successfully woven these spiritual threads into their innovation tapestries, setting new standards for success and responsibility in the corporate world.

Spirituality and Innovation: An Evolving Synergy

Integrating spirituality into business innovation marks the dawn of a new era in corporate strategy and development. This synergy challenges traditional business models, proposing a holistic approach where spiritual values are not seen as separate from, but integral to, the innovative process.

The Role of Mindfulness in Fostering Innovation

Mindfulness, a key tenet of many spiritual practices, involves being fully present and aware in the moment. This heightened awareness can lead to more profound insights and creative problem-solving in a business context.

Enhanced Focus and Clarity: Mindfulness practices help declutter the mind, allowing innovative thinkers to focus deeply on the problem at hand without distraction.

Openness to New Ideas: A mindful approach fosters an openness to new ideas and perspectives, which is essential for groundbreaking innovations.

Empathy: A Catalyst for User-Centric Innovation

Empathy, the ability to understand and share the feelings of others, is crucial in developing innovations that truly resonate with consumers.

Understanding Customer Needs: Empathetic businesses can better understand and anticipate the needs and desires of their customers, leading to more user-centric innovations.

Inclusive Design and Development: Empathy encourages the inclusion of diverse perspectives in the design and development process, resulting in products and services that cater to a broader audience.

Interconnectedness: Weaving a Web of Collaborative Innovation

The spiritual principle of interconnectedness — the understanding that everything is connected — encourages a collaborative approach to innovation.

> **Cross-Functional Teams:** Encouraging collaboration across different functions and departments leads to a more holistic and comprehensive innovation strategy.

> **Partnerships and Community Engagement:** Building partnerships with external communities and stakeholders can provide new insights and drive collective innovation efforts.

Examples of Spiritually-Inspired Innovation in Businesses

A Technology Giant Embracing Mindfulness: Consider a leading technology company that integrates mindfulness into its organizational culture, encouraging employees to engage in meditation and reflective practices, sparking creative technological solutions.

A Retailer Focused on Empathetic Customer Service: A retail business that trains its employees in empathy to better understand and meet customer needs, leading to innovative customer service strategies and a loyal customer base.

 A Manufacturing Company Valuing Interconnectedness: A manufacturing firm that fosters interconnectedness by collaborating with local communities and suppliers, leading to sustainable and community-supported innovations.

The Impact of Spirituality-Infused Innovation

The impact of integrating spirituality into business innovation extends beyond financial gains. It fosters a work environment that values creativity, ethical responsibility, and personal growth.

> **Sustainable and Ethical Business Practices:** Spirituality-infused innovation often leads to more sustainable and ethical business practices, as decisions are made considering their broader impact.

Employee Well-being and Satisfaction: Such an approach enhances employee well-being and job satisfaction, as workers feel aligned with the company's values and purpose.

Long-term Business Success: Businesses that combine spiritual values with innovation tend to enjoy long-term success and resilience, as they are grounded in principles that transcend market fluctuations.

The convergence of spirituality and innovation in business is not just a trend but a fundamental shift towards a more conscious and holistic approach to corporate success. This blend leads to innovations that are not only commercially viable but also spiritually enriching, marking a step towards a more empathetic, mindful, and interconnected business world. In this new landscape, companies that embrace this harmonious blend set new benchmarks for success, characterized by what they achieve and how they achieve it — with integrity, creativity, and a deep sense of purpose.

Cultivating Creativity with a Spiritual Essence: Building a Holistic Workplace Culture

In the contemporary business landscape, a new paradigm is emerging—one where creativity flourishes under the nurturing light of spirituality. This article explores the intricate process of fostering a spiritually-inspired creative culture within the workplace. It delves into practices that empower team members to venture beyond conventional boundaries, embracing new ideas and creative risks, all while remaining harmoniously aligned with the business's spiritual ethos. From establishing spaces for meditation and reflection to embracing diverse perspectives and facilitating open, non-judgmental brainstorming sessions, this journey reveals how spirituality can be a powerful catalyst for creativity and innovation.

The Intersection of Spirituality and Creativity in the Workplace

At the heart of this new cultural shift is the recognition that spirituality and creativity are not disparate entities but interconnected facets of a holistic work environment. A spiritually-inspired creative culture recognizes that every individual is not just an employee but a whole person, whose spiritual and creative aspects are integral to their professional output and satisfaction.

Nurturing Spaces for Meditation and Reflection

Creating Tranquil Spaces: Establishing dedicated spaces for meditation and reflection is a tangible expression of a company's commitment to its employees' spiritual well-being. These tranquil corners, be it a quiet room or a serene corner in the office, provide a sanctuary where employees can retreat, rejuvenate, and reconnect with their inner selves, emerging more focused and creatively charged.

Integrating Mindfulness Practices: Encouraging regular mindfulness practices, such as guided meditations or silent contemplation, can significantly enhance mental clarity and creative thinking. These practices help in quieting the mind, allowing for the emergence of new ideas and perspectives that might otherwise be drowned out in the noise of daily work pressures.

Fostering Diversity and Inclusivity for Broader Perspectives

Embracing diverse perspectives is crucial in a spiritually-inspired creative culture. A workforce that reflects a wide a rray of backgrounds, experiences, and beliefs is more likely to generate many innovative ideas and solutions.

Cultivating an Inclusive Environment: Creating an environment where every voice is valued and every perspective is given due consideration fosters a sense of belonging and leads to a richer, more diverse set of creative ideas. This inclusivity is the bedrock of a spiritually-nurturing and creatively-thriving workplace.

Leveraging Diverse Insights: Encouraging employees to share their unique insights and experiences can lead to breakthrough ideas and innovations. The confluence of different cultural and spiritual backgrounds can be a fertile ground for creative ideation.

Facilitating Open and Non-Judgmental Brainstorming Sessions

Brainstorming sessions in a spiritually-inspired culture are about ideation and creating a space where every idea is welcomed and considered without judgment.

Encouraging Free-Flowing Ideas: These sessions focus on letting ideas flow freely, emphasising quantity and diversity rather than immediate practicality or feasibility. This approach allows for the emergence of unconventional and creative ideas that might be overlooked.

Building on Ideas Collaboratively: Adopting techniques like 'Yes, And' instead of 'Yes, But' encourages team members to build on each other's ideas, fostering a collaborative and supportive environment where creativity can flourish.

Real-World Examples of Spiritually-Inspired Creative Cultures

A Tech Company Embracing Mindfulness: Consider a tech company that has integrated meditation rooms and regular mindfulness sessions into its routine. Employees report feeling more relaxed, focused, and creatively invigorated, leading to the developing innovative software solutions that have set new industry standards.

A Design Firm Valuing Diverse Perspectives: A graphic design firm prioritizes inclusivity and diversity in its hiring practices. The result is a vibrant team culture that produces a range of creative designs, appealing to a broader market due to the diverse insights that fuel their creation.

The journey towards fostering a spiritually-inspired creative culture is both enriching and transformative. It involves reimagining the workplace as a space for business operations and a nurturing ground for the human spirit, where creativity is encouraged and celebrated. In such an environment, innovation becomes more than just an output; it becomes a natural expression of a workforce that feels valued, connected, and spiritually fulfilled. This cultural shift paves the way for businesses to achieve success and contribute to the well-being and growth of their most valuable asset—their people.

Unleashing Creativity Through Mindfulness: A Path to Innovative Thinking

In the fast-paced, constantly evolving business world, creativity is not just a luxury; it's a necessity. But how do we continuously tap into our creative reservoirs, especially under pressure? This article explores the transformative role of mindfulness practices in enhancing creativity and fostering innovative thinking. We delve into how meditation, mindful reflection, and presence can unlock the mind's potential for new ideas and perspectives. We will also examine how these practices help overcome mental blocks, encourage a state of flow, and cultivate open-mindedness – all essential for the creative process.

The Interplay Between Mindfulness and Creativity

Mindfulness and creativity are deeply interconnected. While mindfulness is the practice of being present and fully engaged with whatever we're doing, free from distraction or judgment, creativity is the ability to develop original ideas that have value. By practising mindfulness, we can clear the mental clutter that often hinders our creative thinking.

Meditation: Clearing the Canvas for Creative Thoughts

Meditation is often associated with relaxation and stress reduction, but its benefits extend far into the realms of creativity.

> **Silencing the Inner Critic:** Regular meditation helps in quieting the inner critic that stifles creative thought. In the silence and stillness, the mind is free to wander and explore new ideas without self-judgment.

> **Enhancing Concentration and Focus:** Meditation trains the brain to focus and concentrate. This heightened focus can be directed towards creative tasks, allowing for deeper and more sustained exploration of ideas.

> **Fostering Neural Connections:** Studies have shown that meditation can change brain regions linked to learning and memory processes, emotional regulation, self-referential processing, and perspective-taking. These changes can foster a conducive environment for creative thinking.

Mindful Reflection: A Gateway to New Perspectives

Mindful reflection involves a conscious and deliberate thought process, reflecting on experiences, ideas, and emotions from a stance of curiosity and openness.

Cultivating Curiosity: We encourage a curious and exploratory attitude by reflecting mindfully. This curiosity can lead to questioning norms and exploring uncharted territories in thought – a key driver of creativity.

Connecting Disparate Ideas: Mindful reflection allows us to draw connections between seemingly unrelated ideas, a process at the heart of creative thinking.

Presence: Embracing the Moment for Creative Insights

The practice of being fully present, or in the 'now', can be a powerful catalyst for creativity.

Heightened Awareness: Being present heightens our sensory awareness, making us more receptive to nuances and details that can spark creative ideas.

1. **Reducing Stress and Anxiety:** Presence helps in reducing stress and anxiety, which are often barriers to creative thinking. A relaxed mind is more open to lateral thinking and creative breakthroughs.

Overcoming Mental Blocks Through Mindfulness

Mindfulness practices are particularly effective in overcoming mental blocks, those frustrating barriers that prevent us from accessing our creative potential.

Breaking the Cycle of Overthinking: Mindfulness breaks the cycle of rumination and overthinking, often leading to creative blocks.

Releasing Fixed Mindsets: By fostering open-mindedness, mindfulness helps us let go of fixed mindsets and rigid thinking patterns that limit creative possibilities.

Fostering a State of Flow with Mindfulness

The state of flow, or being 'in the zone', is where creativity often flourishes. Mindfulness practices can significantly enhance our ability to enter this state.

> **Seamless Engagement:** Mindful practices train us to engage in tasks seamlessly without the distraction of external or internal noise, a prerequisite for achieving a flow state.

> **Balancing Skills and Challenges:** Mindfulness helps balance our skills with the challenges at hand, a key aspect of entering and maintaining a flow state.

Incorporating mindfulness into our daily routine is not just a strategy for personal well-being; it's a direct investment in our creative capabilities. By practising meditation, mindful reflection, and presence, we open ourselves to a world of untapped ideas and unexplored possibilities. This approach enhances our ability to think creatively and aligns us more closely with our innermost thoughts and feelings, leading to a more authentic and fulfilling expression of our professional and personal selves.

Harmonizing Spirit and Strategy: Navigating Innovation with Spiritual Integrity

In the dynamic arena of contemporary business, the challenge of harmonizing spiritual values with the relentless drive for competitive innovation is a formidable task. This article delves into the intricate balancing act of fostering innovation while remaining true to one's spiritual ethos in a competitive business environment. It explores how businesses can navigate this balance, ensuring their innovation efforts are effective in maintaining competitiveness and deeply rooted in their spiritual principles. From ethical considerations in the innovation process to maintaining integrity and authenticity and the pivotal role of purpose-driven innovation, this exploration offers strategies to align spiritual values with the demands of modern business.

The Intersection of Spirituality and Competitive Innovation

In a world where the pursuit of innovation often leads to cutthroat competition, aligning these efforts with spiritual values presents both a challenge and an opportunity. It requires a reassessment of what true success means and how it can be achieved without compromising one's core values.

Ethical Considerations in Innovation

Ethical considerations form the backbone of any innovation strategy aligned with spiritual values. This involves ensuring that every innovative step taken is legally compliant and ethically sound, respecting the well-being of all stakeholders involved.

> **Sustainable and Responsible Practices:** Prioritizing sustainable and environmentally friendly practices in innovation efforts ensures that business growth does not come at the planet's or future generations' expense.

> **Stakeholder Welfare:** Ensuring that innovations contribute positively to the welfare of employees, customers, and the broader community aligns business practices with a more profound sense of purpose and responsibility.

Maintaining Integrity and Authenticity

Maintaining integrity and authenticity is crucial for businesses aiming to uphold their spiritual values in the race to stay ahead.

> **Transparent Business Practices:** Conducting business with transparency fosters trust and loyalty among stakeholders, reinforcing the company's commitment to its values.

> **Authentic Brand Messaging:** Ensuring that the brand's messaging and commitments align with its actions strengthens the authenticity of the business.

The Importance of Purpose-Driven Innovation

Innovation driven by a clear, purposeful mission transcends the pursuit of profit, anchoring business growth in a meaningful context.

> **Aligning Innovation with Mission:** Innovations should be closely aligned with the business's mission and vision, ensuring that they contribute to the company's broader purpose.

Impact Beyond Profit: Measuring the success of innovations not just by their financial return but also by their impact on societal and environmental welfare reflects a commitment to a higher purpose.

Navigating Challenges in Balancing Spiritual Values and Innovation

The path to balancing spiritual values with competitive innovation is fraught with challenges that require strategic navigation.

Resisting Short-Term Temptations: Staying true to long-term spiritual values often means resisting short-term gains that contradict these principles.

Cultivating a Patient Approach: A patient approach to innovation that values thorough research and considers long-term implications is critical in maintaining this balance.

Examples of Balancing Spiritual Values and Innovation

A Tech Company Prioritizing Ethical AI: Consider a tech company developing artificial intelligence solutions. They balance innovative advancement with moral responsibility by prioritizing ethical considerations, such as transparency and fairness, in their AI development.

A Fashion Brand Embracing Sustainable Practices: A fashion brand that innovates by creating sustainable, eco-friendly clothing lines exemplifies a commitment to innovation that respects environmental conservation and ethical consumerism.

In the quest for innovative excellence, embedding spiritual values into the fabric of business strategies offers a path to sustainable, ethical, and meaningful success. This approach fosters a competitive edge and nurtures a corporate ethos resonant with integrity, responsibility, and purpose. Balancing spiritual values with competitive innovation is not just about achieving business goals; it's about redefining the very goals themselves, aspiring to a vision of success that uplifts the company and the community and environment it inhabits. In this harmonious blend of spirit and strategy, businesses find commercial success, a deeper fulfilment, and a lasting, positive impact on the world.

Ch 8. Ethical Entrepreneurship: Navigating business challenges with integrity

In the dynamic tapestry of modern entrepreneurship, the quest to navigate business challenges with unwavering integrity is more than a noble aspiration; it is a vital necessity. Chapter 8, "Ethical Entrepreneurship: Navigating Business Challenges with Integrity," delves into the intricate interplay between ethical decision-making and entrepreneurial success. This chapter serves as a guiding light for entrepreneurs who aspire to blend commercial success with moral rectitude, navigating the often murky waters of the business world without losing sight of their core values and spiritual principles.

The Essence of Ethical Entrepreneurship

The journey of ethical entrepreneurship begins with a fundamental understanding of what it means to operate a business grounded in integrity. This exploration goes beyond the conventional parameters of profit and loss, delving into the heart of ethical conduct in business. It is a journey that redefines success, viewing it not just in terms of financial gain but as a measure of how business practices align with moral and spiritual values.

The Balancing Act: Profit and Principles

At the core of ethical entrepreneurship lies the delicate balance between profitability and adherence to ethical principles. This section discusses entrepreneurs' challenges in aligning their business objectives with their moral compass. It highlights strategies for making decisions that serve the business's financial interests without compromising ethical standards. From pricing and marketing to engaging with competitors, this chapter outlines how to maintain integrity in the face of commercial pressures.

Navigating Ethical Dilemmas

Entrepreneurs often encounter situations where the right action is not black and white. This segment delves into common ethical dilemmas in business, such as managing conflicts of interest, fair practices in supply chain management, and dealing with challenging employee issues. Here, readers will find practical guidance on making tough decisions that uphold ethical standards, supported by real-life examples of businesses that have successfully navigated these dilemmas.

Creating an Ethical Business Culture

Establishing and nurturing an ethical culture within a business is pivotal to ensuring integrity permeating every level of the organization. This section explores the role of leadership in fostering an ethical climate, techniques to encourage ethical behaviour among employees, and the implementation of policies and training that reinforce ethical standards. It also discusses how businesses can measure and sustain their ethical practices over time and appropriately address any lapses in ethical conduct.

Real-World Examples of Ethical Entrepreneurship

Throughout the chapter, stories and case studies of businesses and entrepreneurs who have successfully integrated ethical practices into their operations provide inspiration and practical insights. These examples showcase a variety of industries and the unique ways in which ethical entrepreneurship can manifest, offering readers tangible models to emulate.

The Path Ahead for Ethical Entrepreneurs

As the chapter unfolds, it becomes evident that ethical entrepreneurship is not just a strategy but a holistic approach to business. It involves making decisions that reflect economic rationality and a deep commitment to doing what is right. The journey of an ethical entrepreneur is marked by constant learning, adaptation, and a steadfast commitment to values that transcend the pursuit of profit.

Ethical entrepreneurship represents a beacon of hope and a path to transformation in the business world. It proves that business success and ethical conduct are not mutually exclusive but are, in fact, synergistic. For those who embark on this journey, the rewards are manifold – not just in terms of financial success but also in the fulfilment that comes from knowing that their business practices contribute positively to society and align with their deepest spiritual values. As we turn the pages of this chapter, we are invited to re-envision the role of the entrepreneur – not just as a businessperson but as a custodian of ethical integrity and a visionary forging a path toward a more just and principled world.

Ethical Entrepreneurship: Redefining Success in the Modern Business World

Ethical entrepreneurship has become more relevant than ever in an era where business dynamics are continuously evolving. This article explores the essence of ethical entrepreneurship in the modern world, seeking to understand its principles, significance, and application in the contemporary business landscape. It sheds light on the evolution of ethical standards, the growing emphasis on corporate social responsibility, and the profound impact of ethical practices on long-term business success.

The Foundation of Ethical Entrepreneurship

Ethical entrepreneurship goes beyond mere compliance with laws and regulations. It represents a commitment to conducting business with integrity, fairness, and respect for people and the planet.

Principles of Ethical Decision-Making: Central to ethical entrepreneurship is the decision-making process that considers all stakeholders' welfare. This involves evaluating the impact of business decisions on employees, customers, the community, and the environment.

Integrity in Business involves adhering to moral and ethical principles ensuring honesty and transparency in all business dealings. It's about doing the right thing, even when it's not the easiest or most profitable path.

Application in Entrepreneurship: Applying these principles means embedding ethical considerations into every aspect of the business, from product development and marketing to supply chain management and customer service.

Evolution of Ethical Standards in Business

Over the years, there has been a significant shift in the way businesses approach ethics and responsibility.

From Profit to Purpose: The traditional business model focused primarily on profit maximization. However, a paradigm has shifted towards a more purpose-driven approach, where businesses seek to make a positive impact while being profitable.

Rise of Corporate Social Responsibility (CSR): CSR has evolved from a peripheral activity to a core business strategy. It reflects a company's commitment to contribute to economic development while improving the quality of life of the workforce and their families, as well as the local community and society at large.

The Increasing Importance of Corporate Social Responsibility

CSR has become an integral part of modern business strategy, reflecting a company's commitment to operate economically, socially, and environmentally sustainably.

Environmental Sustainability: This includes initiatives to reduce carbon footprints, manage waste, and utilize renewable energy sources, reflecting a responsibility towards ecological stewardship.

Social Welfare: Many companies now engage in activities that support community welfare, ranging from educational programs to healthcare initiatives.

Economic Responsibility: Ethical businesses also focus on contributing to the economy in a way that benefits society, which includes fair wages, ethical sourcing, and supporting local suppliers.

Impact of Ethical Practices on Long-Term Success

Adopting ethical business practices is not only about doing good; it has a tangible impact on long-term success.

Building Trust and Reputation: Ethical practices help build trust with customers, employees, and stakeholders. This trust is a crucial component of a strong brand reputation, which, in turn, drives customer loyalty and business growth.

Attracting and Retaining Talent: A commitment to ethics and responsibility makes a company more attractive to potential employees and helps retain existing talent who value working for a purpose-driven organization.

Sustainable Growth: Ethical businesses tend to experience sustainable growth because they consider the long-term implications of their actions, rather than seeking short-term gains.

In today's business environment, ethical entrepreneurship is not just a moral choice but a strategic imperative. By embedding ethical considerations into their core business strategies, entrepreneurs can build companies that thrive economically and contribute positively to society and the environment. This harmonious blend of profit and purpose creates a business landscape that is more equitable, sustainable, resilient, and innovative. Ethical entrepreneurship, therefore, represents a powerful and inspiring model for redefining success in the modern business world.

Ethics and Earnings: Striking a Balance in Ethical Entrepreneurship

In the complex world of modern business, ethical entrepreneurs face the daunting task of harmonizing profit-making with their core principles. This challenge goes beyond mere compliance with ethical standards; it is about embedding these standards into the very DNA of the business. This article delves into the strategies for aligning business goals with ethical standards, highlighting the approaches to ethical pricing, marketing, and competition and balancing investor expectations with a commitment to ethical practices. Through case studies of companies that have successfully walked this tightrope, we explore the practicalities of maintaining integrity while ensuring profitability in the business world.

Understanding the Balance Between Profit and Principles

The pursuit of profit, often viewed as the primary objective of any business, can sometimes conflict with ethical principles. The key is to find a balance where business goals do not overshadow ethical considerations.

Strategies for Aligning Business Goals with Ethical Standards

> **Establishing Clear Ethical Guidelines:** Developing a clear set of ethical guidelines helps make decisions that align with business objectives and ethical commitments.

> **Integrating Ethics into Business Models:** Creating business models that inherently incorporate ethical practices ensures that profit-making and ethical standards are not mutually exclusive.

Ethical Pricing: Balancing Fairness and Profitability

Ethical pricing involves setting prices that are fair to consumers and sustainable for the business.

> **Cost-Based Pricing:** This approach involves setting prices based on the cost of production plus a fair margin, ensuring that the price reflects the true value of the product or service.

> **Value-Based Pricing:** Value-based pricing is about setting prices based on the perceived value to the customer, balancing customer satisfaction with profitability.

Ethical Marketing: Promoting with Integrity

Marketing in an ethical manner involves transparency and honesty in advertising and promotions.

> **Truthful Advertising:** Ensuring that marketing campaigns are truthful and do not mislead consumers.

> **Socially Responsible Marketing:** Engaging in marketing practices considering the societal impact and promoting positive messages.

Ethical Competition: Succeeding with Honor

Competing ethically involves respecting the market, competitors, and consumers.

> **Respect for Competitors:** Engaging in fair competition, avoiding practices like price undercutting or false advertising that harm competitors.

Consumer Rights and Fair Play: Respecting consumer rights and engaging in practices that promote fair play in the market.

Managing Investor Expectations Ethically

Balancing investor expectations with ethical commitments can be challenging but is essential for long-term sustainability.

Transparent Communication: Keeping investors informed about the ethical standards of the business and how they align with long-term profitability.

Demonstrating Long-Term Value: Showing investors how ethical practices can lead to sustainable growth and long-term value creation.

The journey of balancing profit and principles in business is intricate and challenging but deeply rewarding. It requires a commitment to uphold ethical standards at every turn and a willingness to innovate in aligning these standards with business goals. The case studies of companies that have successfully managed this balance serve as a testament that ethical entrepreneurship is feasible and profitable in the long run. By championing ethical practices, businesses can build trust and loyalty with their customers and stakeholders, paving the way for sustainable growth and success. This balance is not just a business strategy but a commitment to a higher purpose, ensuring that the pursuit of profit does not compromise the core values that define the spirit of true entrepreneurship.

Ethical Decision-Making in Business: Steering Through Moral Complexities

In the intricate world of entrepreneurship, ethical dilemmas are an inescapable reality. These dilemmas often place entrepreneurs at a crossroads where business acumen seemingly diverges from the road of moral righteousness. This article delves into entrepreneurs' common ethical dilemmas and offers a comprehensive framework for navigating these challenges. By exploring conflicts of interest, ethical considerations in supply chain management, and tough choices affecting various stakeholders, we aim to establish a decision-making process that harmonizes business savvy with moral integrity.

Understanding Ethical Dilemmas in Entrepreneurship

Ethical dilemmas in business are situations where decisions have significant moral implications, often involving a choice between competing values or principles.

The Nature of Ethical Dilemmas: These dilemmas often involve situations where the right course of action is unclear, and stakeholders may have conflicting interests or values.

Common Ethical Challenges: Entrepreneurs frequently encounter dilemmas related to conflicts of interest, fairness in treatment, transparency, and social responsibility.

Framework for Navigating Ethical Dilemmas

A structured approach is essential for effectively navigating ethical dilemmas.

Identifying Ethical Issues: The first step is clearly identifying the ethical issues involved in the decision-making scenario.

Assessing Stakeholder Impacts: Consider the impact of potential decisions on all stakeholders, including employees, customers, suppliers, and the broader community.

Evaluating Options: Weigh the pros and cons of each option, considering both ethical implications and business outcomes.

Conflicts of Interest: Managing with Integrity

Conflicts of interest are situations where personal interests or external pressures may influence professional judgment.

Disclosure and Transparency: The key to managing conflicts of interest lies in full disclosure and maintaining transparency with all concerned parties.

Separating Personal and Professional: Implementing strict policies to separate personal interests from business decisions is critical to avoid biases.

Ethical Considerations in Supply Chain Management

Ethical supply chain management involves ensuring that business practices are fair, sustainable, and socially responsible at every supply chain step.

Responsible Sourcing: This includes ensuring that materials and products are sourced ethically, respecting environmental standards and labour rights.

Supplier Relations: Building strong, ethical relationships with suppliers based on mutual respect and fair practices.

Making Tough Choices: Balancing Business and Ethics

Difficult decisions often involve balancing the interests of the business against ethical considerations.

Layoffs and Employee Treatment: Decisions related to employee layoffs and treatment require a careful balance between financial necessities and the moral obligation to treat employees fairly.

Customer Interests: Ensuring that business decisions do not unfairly disadvantage or exploit customers is crucial for long-term success and reputation.

Real-World Examples: Ethical Decision-Making in Action

A Retail Giant's Ethical Sourcing Initiative: A global retail company implementing a policy to only source products from suppliers that adhere to strict environmental and labour standards.

A Tech Company's Transparent Handling of a Data Breach: A technology firm facing a data breach that proactively and transparently communicates with affected customers, taking full responsibility and offering remedies.

Navigating ethical dilemmas in business decisions requires a delicate balance between commercial objectives and moral imperatives. By adopting a structured approach to ethical decision-making, entrepreneurs can ensure that their business practices yield financial success and reflect their commitment to moral responsibility. As demonstrated by numerous real-world examples, ethical entrepreneurship is not just about making the right decisions but about setting a standard for conducting business. It is about building a legacy of integrity and trust that transcends financial metrics and contributes to a more equitable and responsible business ecosystem.

Cultivating Integrity: The Blueprint for an Ethical Business Culture

In modern business, establishing a culture that inherently promotes ethical behaviour is both challenging and necessary. This article explores the multifaceted approach to building and sustaining an ethical business culture. It delves into the crucial role of leadership in setting ethical standards, the strategies to foster ethical behaviour among employees, and the mechanisms to institutionalize these practices through policies and training. Furthermore, it addresses the ongoing process of maintaining ethical standards over time and effectively responding to ethical breaches when they occur.

Foundation of an Ethical Business Culture

An ethical business culture is rooted in the core values of the organization. It transcends written codes of conduct to become an intrinsic part of the daily operations and interactions within the company.

Role of Leadership in Ethical Culture: Leaders play a pivotal role in setting the tone for an ethical culture. Their actions, decisions, and communication set a precedent for acceptable behaviour within the organization.

Aligning Values with Actions: An essential aspect of building an ethical culture is ensuring that the company's stated values align with actual practices. This congruence between words and actions reinforces the authenticity of the organization's commitment to ethics.

Encouraging Ethical Behaviour Among Employees

Creating an environment where ethical behaviour is the norm involves more than just establishing rules; it requires fostering a mindset where employees naturally consider the moral implications of their actions.

Ethical Training and Awareness: Regular training sessions on ethics and compliance help employees understand the importance of moral behaviour and the specific expectations of the organization.

Open Dialogue and Communication: Encouraging open discussions about ethical dilemmas and grey areas helps employees feel more comfortable and prepared to handle such situations.

Recognition and Reinforcement: Recognizing and rewarding ethical behaviour reinforces its value and encourages others to follow suit.

Institutionalizing Ethical Practices

Ethical behaviour must be institutionalized through clear policies and consistent practices to become ingrained in a company's culture.

Developing Comprehensive Policies: Clear policies provide guidelines for expected behaviour and the consequences of unethical actions.

Regular Audits and Assessments: Conducting regular audits and assessments of ethical practices helps identify improvement areas and ensures compliance with ethical standards.

Maintaining Ethical Standards Over Time

Maintaining high ethical standards is an ongoing process that requires continuous effort and adaptation.

Regular Reviews and Updates: Regularly reviewing and updating ethical policies and practices ensure that they remain relevant and effective.

Staying Abreast of Legal and Social Changes: Keeping up-to-date with changes in laws and societal expectations is crucial for maintaining an ethically responsible business.

Responding to Ethical Breaches

Despite best efforts, ethical breaches may occur. The response to these incidents is critical in upholding the integrity of the business.

Immediate and Transparent Action: Addressing ethical breaches quickly and transparently demonstrates the company's commitment to its ethical standards.

Learning and Improvement: Analyzing ethical breaches to understand how they occurred and implementing measures to prevent future incidents is key to strengthening the ethical culture.

Building and sustaining an ethical business culture is a dynamic and multifaceted endeavour. It requires a clear vision from leadership, a commitment to aligning values with actions, and implementing practical measures to ensure these values are reflected in every aspect of the business. An ethical culture fortifies the organization's integrity, enhances its reputation, fosters trust among stakeholders, and contributes to long-term success. By embedding ethical considerations into the fabric of the organizational culture, businesses can navigate the complexities of the modern market with a strong moral compass, setting an example for others to follow.

Ch 9. Sustainable Practices: Aligning business operations with spiritual and environmental consciousness

This chapter embarks on an enlightening journey into the heart of modern business ethics. It explores the vital intersection where environmental sustainability meets spiritual awareness. At this point, business operations transcend mere profit and contribute meaningfully to the planet's health and the welfare of its inhabitants. This chapter is not just about strategies and policies; it's a deep dive into a philosophy that integrates environmental responsibility with spiritual values, fostering a business model that is not only viable but also virtuous and visionary.

Embracing a New Paradigm in Business

The era we live in demands a transformation in how we perceive and conduct business. Gone are the days when environmental considerations were an afterthought. Today, they are at the forefront of business planning and execution. This section discusses why and how businesses must align their operations with a commitment to environmental sustainability underpinned by a strong spiritual ethos.

The Philosophy Behind Sustainable Business Practices

> **Interconnectedness of Life:** Interconnectedness is rooted in various spiritual traditions — the understanding that all life forms are connected and that our actions have far-reaching consequences. This idea forms the foundation of sustainable business practices.

> **From Profit to Purpose:** Moving beyond profit as the sole purpose of business, this new philosophy emphasizes purpose, which includes caring for the environment and uplifting communities.

Implementing Eco-Friendly Business Processes

Transitioning to sustainable operations is a practical and necessary step for modern businesses. This part of the chapter outlines actionable strategies for businesses to become more eco-friendly.

Reducing Carbon Footprint: Simple yet effective strategies for reducing a business's carbon footprint, such as energy-efficient lighting, machinery, and digital rather than physical processes.

Waste Management and Recycling: Innovative waste management and recycling practices that not only reduce environmental impact but also often result in cost savings.

Sustainable Supply Chain Management: A Holistic Approach

A sustainable supply chain is crucial for a genuinely environmentally-conscious business. This section focuses on how companies can ensure their supply chains are sustainable, ethical, and align with their spiritual values.

Ethical Sourcing: Ensuring that products and materials are sourced in an environmentally sustainable and socially responsible manner.

Collaboration with Suppliers: Building partnerships with suppliers who are committed to sustainability and ethical practices.

Stakeholder Engagement in Sustainability Efforts

Engaging stakeholders is vital to the successful implementation of sustainable practices. This part discusses how businesses can involve various stakeholders in their sustainability journey.

Employee Participation: Encouraging employees to participate in and contribute to sustainability initiatives, creating a sense of ownership and commitment.

Customer Education and Engagement: Educating customers about the company's sustainability efforts and how they can contribute, thereby building a community of environmentally-conscious consumers.

In today's world, aligning business operations with spiritual and environmental consciousness is not just an ethical choice, but a strategic necessity. This chapter provides a comprehensive guide to doing business in a way that honors our planet and its inhabitants, ensuring that companies contribute positively to the world while still achieving their commercial objectives. By embedding sustainable practices into their core, businesses can build a more conscientious, responsible, and sustainable future.

Spirituality Meets Sustainability: The Ethos of Conscious Business

A profound shift is occurring in the contemporary business world - a movement towards integrating spirituality and environmentalism into the core of business operations. This article delves into the philosophical foundations of sustainable business practices, exploring how the interconnectedness of all life, a fundamental spiritual concept, becomes crucial in fostering environmental stewardship within the business arena. We will examine how spiritual principles such as mindfulness, compassion, and stewardship are not just abstract concepts but can be practically applied to nurture and respect our environment through business practices.

The Spiritual Roots of Environmental Stewardship

At the heart of sustainable business practices lies a deep-seated recognition of the interconnectedness of all life. This perspective, rooted in various spiritual traditions, sees the earth and its resources not as mere commodities but as sacred entities that deserve respect and care.

> **Understanding Interconnectedness:** This concept teaches that every action in business has a ripple effect, impacting the environment and all living beings. This understanding is key to realizing the broader implications of business decisions on the planet's health.

> **Integrating Spiritual Values:** Values like mindfulness, compassion, and respect for all forms of life become essential in guiding business decisions, ensuring they contribute positively to the environment and society.

Translating Spiritual Principles into Business Practices

Translating spiritual principles into business practices represents a paradigm shift from traditional profit-centred models to a more holistic approach.

> **Mindfulness in Business Operations:** Implementing mindfulness in business involves being fully present and aware of the impact of every business decision. It means

considering the long-term environmental effects of business activities.

Compassion Towards the Environment: Compassion in business translates to actions that consider the environment's well-being, such as reducing carbon footprints, minimizing waste, and using sustainable materials.

Stewardship and Sustainable Growth: Embracing stewardship in business means taking responsibility for the environmental impact of business activities. It involves pursuing growth in harmony with nature, ensuring that business practices do not deplete or harm natural resources.

Practical Applications of Spiritual and Environmental Principles

The practical application of these spiritual and environmental principles involves concrete steps and strategies that businesses can adopt.

Sustainable Resource Management: This includes using resources responsibly, opting for renewable resources, and implementing recycling and conservation practices in daily operations.

Ethical Supply Chains: Ensuring the supply chain adheres to ethical standards, including fair labour practices and environmentally friendly sourcing.

Green Innovation Investing in research and development to create products and services that are environmentally friendly and contribute to sustainable living.

The integration of spirituality and environmentalism in business represents a radical rethinking of the traditional business model. It proposes a world where businesses operate with a consciousness that transcends profit, where every decision is made with mindfulness and compassion towards the environment. This approach leads to sustainable business practices and fosters a deeper sense of purpose and fulfilment in the business world. By grounding their operations in this spiritual and environmental ethos, businesses can contribute to a more sustainable and equitable world, creating a legacy that goes beyond financial success to include environmental well-being and spiritual enrichment.

Eco-Innovation in Action: Crafting Green Operations for Sustainable Business

In an era marked by a growing consciousness about environmental sustainability, businesses across the globe are increasingly turning to green operations. This shift is not just about adhering to environmental norms but is a strategic move towards more responsible, efficient, and ultimately sustainable business practices. This article explores the various facets of implementing eco-friendly practices in business operations, covering the spectrum from waste reduction and energy conservation to the use of sustainable materials and green manufacturing processes. Alongside the environmental benefits, we delve into how these practices can lead to cost savings and efficiency gains. Highlighting examples from businesses that have successfully embraced green operations, this piece paints a comprehensive picture of how eco-friendly strategies can be seamlessly integrated into the business fabric, contributing to a model that is both sustainable and spiritually aligned.

The Shift to Green Operations

The move towards green operations is driven by the dual need to minimize environmental impact and adapt to changing market demands and regulatory landscapes.

Reducing Waste: A Key Pillar of Green Operations

> **Waste Minimization Strategies:** Implementing practices such as recycling, composting, and reusing materials. This not only reduces the environmental footprint but also lowers operational costs.

> **Lean Management Principles:** Adopting lean management principles to streamline processes and reduce waste generation at the source.

Energy Conservation: Harnessing Efficiency

Energy conservation is a critical aspect of green operations, with both environmental and economic benefits.

Energy-Efficient Technologies: Upgrading to energy-efficient technologies, such as LED lighting, energy-efficient appliances, and smart systems, to reduce energy consumption.

Renewable Energy Sources: Transitioning to renewable energy sources like solar, wind, or hydroelectric power to reduce reliance on fossil fuels.

Sustainable Materials: The Backbone of Green Manufacturing

Choosing sustainable materials is essential for reducing the environmental impact of products and operations.

Eco-friendly Material Selection: Opt for recyclable, biodegradable, or derived from sustainable sources.

Supply Chain Sustainability: Ensuring that materials are sourced from suppliers who adhere to sustainable practices.

Green Manufacturing Processes: Innovating for Sustainability

Green manufacturing involves redesigning production processes to minimize environmental impact.

Eco-efficient Production: Implementing production processes that consume less energy and water, produce fewer emissions, and generate less waste.

Closed-loop Systems: Developing closed-loop systems where waste from one process is used as input for another creating a circular economy model.

The Business Case for Green Operations

Implementing eco-friendly practices in business operations is an environmental imperative and a strategic business decision.

Cost Savings: Energy-efficient practices and waste reduction lead to significant cost savings, offsetting the initial investment over time.

Increased Efficiency: Streamlined processes and efficient use of resources enhance overall operational efficiency.

> **Brand Reputation and Customer Loyalty:** Companies with strong sustainability practices often enjoy a better brand reputation and increased customer loyalty.

The transformation into a business model that prioritizes green operations is both a response to the environmental challenges of our time and a strategic move towards long-term sustainability. By integrating eco-friendly practices into their daily operations, businesses are contributing positively to the environment and reaping benefits in terms of cost savings, efficiency, and enhanced brand image. This approach to business operations showcases a harmony between environmental responsibility and economic pragmatism, setting a precedent for a future where business and sustainability go hand in hand.

Sustainable Supply Chain Management: A Catalyst for Ethical Business Growth

In today's globalized economy, the significance of sustainable supply chain management cannot be overstated. It stands at the forefront of shaping ethical and environmentally responsible business practices. This article examines the critical role of supply chain management in fostering sustainable business operations. It delves into how companies can ensure their supply chains align with environmental and social responsibility goals, including selecting ethical suppliers, ensuring fair labour practices, and reducing the ecological impact of logistics and transportation. Additionally, it addresses the challenges inherent in maintaining a sustainable supply chain, such as adhering to certification processes, ensuring compliance, and nurturing long-term relationships with like-minded suppliers.

Redefining Supply Chain Management for Sustainability

The traditional supply chain model, primarily focused on efficiency and cost reduction, is radically transforming. Modern businesses are now redefining supply chain management with a strong emphasis on sustainability.

Environmental and Social Responsibility in the Supply Chain

> **Choosing Ethical Suppliers:** The selection of suppliers who adhere to sustainable practices is crucial. It evaluates

their commitment to environmental protection, ethical labour practices, and quality assurance.

Ensuring Fair Labour Practices: Ensuring fair labour conditions throughout the supply chain is a moral imperative. This includes safeguarding against child labour, forced labour and ensuring fair wages and safe working conditions.

Eco-friendly Logistics and Transportation: Minimizing the environmental impact of logistics and transportation is integral to a sustainable supply chain. This includes optimizing routes for fuel efficiency, using eco-friendly packaging, and exploring renewable energy sources for transportation.

Overcoming Challenges in Sustainable Supply Chain Management

Managing a sustainable supply chain comes with unique challenges that require strategic planning and commitment.

Certification Processes and Compliance: Navigating various certification processes, such as Fair Trade or ISO standards, is complex but essential for ensuring compliance with sustainability standards.

Monitoring and Ensuring Compliance: It is crucial to regularly monitor suppliers and ensure they adhere to agreed-upon sustainability criteria. This may involve audits, regular reporting, and collaborative initiatives to help suppliers meet standards.

Building Long-term Supplier Relationships: Building long-term relationships with suppliers with similar sustainability values fosters mutual growth and sustainability goals.

Innovations in Sustainable Supply Chain Practices

Technology and process management innovations are pivotal in advancing sustainable supply chain practices.

Blockchain for Transparency: Utilizing blockchain technology in supply chain management enhances transparency and traceability, ensuring that each product's journey can be monitored for ethical compliance.

AI and Data Analytics: Leveraging AI and data analytics to optimize supply chain processes helps reduce waste, improve resource management, and predict supply chain risks.

Real-World Examples of Sustainable Supply Chain Management

A Global Retailer's Ethical Sourcing Initiative: A multinational retail corporation implemented a robust ethical sourcing program, auditing suppliers for environmental and social compliance, and significantly improved their global supply chain sustainability.

A Fashion Brand's Commitment to Fair Labour Practices: An international fashion brand transformed its supply chain by ensuring fair labour practices across all its manufacturing units, setting a new industry standard for ethical fashion.

A Tech Company's Green Logistics Strategy: A technology firm redesigned its logistics strategy to reduce carbon emissions, incorporating electric vehicles for last-mile deliveries and using renewable energy in warehouses.

Sustainable supply chain management represents a fundamental shift in how companies view their role in the global market. It is no longer sufficient to focus solely on efficiency and profit; businesses must also consider their operations' environmental and social impact. By implementing sustainable practices throughout their supply chains, companies contribute positively to the environment and society and build resilience, improve brand reputation, and drive long-term profitability. This approach symbolizes a commitment to ethical business growth, where success is measured financially and by the positive impact on the world and future generations.

Creating a Sustainable Symphony: Engaging Stakeholders in the Green Journey

In the quest for sustainability, stakeholders – employees, customers, investors, and the community – are pivotal. This article explores the multifaceted strategies businesses can employ to engage and educate these key groups in their sustainability efforts. By initiating awareness campaigns, participatory initiatives, and transparent reporting, companies can strengthen their sustainable practices and foster a community that shares spiritual and environmental values. This engagement is more than a corporate responsibility; it's a powerful catalyst for innovation and a sustainable future.

The Cornerstone of Sustainability: Stakeholder Engagement

Sustainability in business is not a solitary journey. It requires the active participation and support of every stakeholder connected to the company.

Engaging Employees in Sustainability Efforts

Employees are the driving force behind any successful sustainability initiative. Their active involvement is crucial for the implementation of sustainable practices.

> **Training and Awareness Programs:** Conducting regular training sessions and workshops to educate employees about sustainability and its importance. This can range from environmental conservation techniques to sustainable work practices.

> **Encouraging Green Ideas and Innovations:** Creating platforms where employees can propose eco-friendly ideas and solutions. This fosters a culture of innovation and empowers employees to contribute to the company's sustainability goals.

Involving Customers in the Sustainability Dialogue

Customers are increasingly conscious of the environmental impact of their purchasing decisions. Engaging them can amplify a company's sustainability efforts.

> **Sustainability Marketing and Communication:** Utilizing marketing and communication channels to educate customers on the company's sustainability initiatives and how they can contribute.

> **Encouraging Sustainable Consumer Practices:** Promoting products and services that encourage sustainable

consumer behaviour, such as reusable packaging or energy-efficient products.

Educating and Collaborating with Investors on Sustainability

Investors play a key role in driving a company's sustainability agenda. Keeping them informed and involved is essential.

Transparent Sustainability Reporting: Regularly reporting on sustainability performance to investors, highlighting achievements, challenges, and future goals.

Showcasing the Long-term Value of Sustainability: Demonstrating how sustainability initiatives contribute to long-term business value, risk mitigation, and brand enhancement.

Community Engagement for Collective Impact

Local communities are often the most impacted by a company's operations. Engaging with them can lead to more impactful and community-oriented sustainability initiatives.

Community-based Sustainability Projects: Partnering with local communities on sustainability projects such as tree planting, waste management, or education programs.

Sustainability Awareness Campaigns: Conduct awareness campaigns in the community to educate and involve them in environmental conservation efforts.

Leveraging Stakeholder Engagement for Innovation

Engaging stakeholders in sustainability is not just about fulfilling corporate responsibility; it's about unlocking new ideas and pathways for sustainable growth.

Feedback Loops for Continuous Improvement: Establishing feedback mechanisms where stakeholders can provide insights and suggestions on sustainability practices.

Collaborative Sustainability Ventures: Collaborating with other businesses, NGOs, or governmental bodies on sustainability projects can lead to innovative solutions and greater impact.

Real-world Examples of Stakeholder Engagement in Sustainability

> **A Retail Giant's Green Consumer Program:** A global retail company that launched a consumer program promoting the use of reusable bags, significantly reducing plastic waste and engaging customers in its sustainability mission.

> **An Energy Company's Community Solar Projects:** An energy company that partnered with local communities to set up community solar projects, providing clean energy and involving the community in renewable energy initiatives.

Engaging stakeholders in sustainability efforts is critical in building a more environmentally conscious and spiritually aligned business model. This engagement is not merely about meeting targets but creating a shared vision for a sustainable future. Businesses can build a robust sustainability ecosystem by actively involving employees, customers, investors, and the community. This collective effort strengthens the company's sustainability initiatives and contributes to a larger movement towards a greener, more responsible world. Through this approach, businesses can create a ripple effect, inspiring change and innovation far beyond their immediate sphere of influence.

Part IV: Expanding Impact and Influence

Ch 10. Networking with Purpose: Building meaningful, spiritually-aligned connections

This chapter begins an insightful journey into redefining networking, traditionally seen as a fundamental element in business. It explores how these essential connections can surpass their usual boundaries, evolving into more meaningful and spiritually-aligned engagements. It is an invitation to delve into a more profound, purpose-driven approach to building relationships in the business realm. This chapter is not merely about expanding your contact list; it's about creating connections that resonate with your spiritual ethos and ethical beliefs. Here, networking is reimagined as a pathway to form relationships rich in mutual growth, shared values, and meaningful engagement – far beyond the superficial transactional exchanges often associated with traditional networking. This introduction aims to unfold the layers of spiritually-aligned networking, illustrating how it is rooted in authenticity, mutual respect, and a shared commitment to higher purposes, significantly contributing to personal and professional enrichment.

Redefining Networking in the Spiritual and Business Context

The chapter begins by redefining the concept of networking in the context of spiritual and business alignment. It delves into what it means to network with purpose, going beyond the conventional business-oriented approach to embrace a perspective that integrates spiritual values.

> **A New Paradigm of Networking:** Moving away from the traditional view of networking as a means to an end, this section emphasizes building connections that align with one's spiritual and ethical values.

> **The Synergy of Spiritual Values and Business Networking:** Discuss how integrating spiritual values like honesty, empathy, and compassion into networking can transform professional relationships into sources of mutual inspiration and growth.

Authenticity: The Core of Spiritually-Aligned Networking

The chapter emphasizes authenticity as the cornerstone of spiritually-aligned networking, highlighting its importance in forging genuine and lasting connections.

Being True to Oneself and Others: Encouraging readers to present themselves authentically, aligning their professional persona with their actual values and beliefs.

Seeking Authentic Relationships: Advices on identifying and connecting with individuals and organizations that genuinely resonate with one's values rather than pursuing superficial interactions.

Cultivating Mutual Respect in Professional Relationships

This section explores the importance of mutual respect in networking, advocating for relationships based on equality, understanding, and a mutual appreciation of each other's values and contributions.

Respecting Diverse Perspectives: Understanding and embracing diversity in professional networks, recognizing that different viewpoints and backgrounds enrich the networking experience.

Building Equitable and Supportive Networks: Strategies for fostering networks where support and respect are mutual, and relationships are not dominated by one-sided benefits.

Shared Commitment to Higher Goals in Networking

The chapter discusses how spiritually-aligned networking often involves a shared commitment to broader goals that extend beyond individual or organizational success.

Aligning with Purpose-Driven Individuals and Organizations: The importance of connecting with people and organizations committed to positively impacting their communities or industries.

Networking for Social and Environmental Impact: Examples of how purpose-driven networking can lead to collaborative efforts in social responsibility and environmental stewardship.

Intentionality in Building and Nurturing Connections

A significant focus of the chapter is on the intentionality behind networking efforts, emphasizing the quality of connections over mere quantity.

Mindful Networking Strategies: Guidance on intentionally seeking and nurturing relationships that align with one's personal and professional growth objectives.

Long-Term Relationship Building: Tips on maintaining and deepening connections over time, turning them into meaningful, long-lasting relationships.

Real-World Examples of Spiritually-Aligned Networking

The chapter brings to life the concept of spiritually-aligned networking with real-world examples and case studies.

A Business Leader's Network for Sustainable Practices: A case study of a business leader whose network promotes sustainable practices within their industry.

A Community-Oriented Networking Group: An example of a networking group that focuses on community development and social entrepreneurship, fostering connections that are geared towards societal improvement.

In "Networking with Purpose: Building Meaningful, Spiritually-Aligned Connections," readers are invited to journey through the transformative process of building a network that supports business growth and resonates with their inner values and aspirations. This chapter provides the tools and insights necessary to navigate the realm of professional networking with a renewed perspective – one that harmonizes the pursuit of business success with the principles of spiritual and ethical integrity. Through this approach, networking becomes an enriching experience, opening doors to relationships that are both professionally rewarding, personally fulfilling, and spiritually resonant.

Cultivating Connections with Purpose: The Art of Spiritually-Aligned Networking

In the dynamic business world, networking is often perceived as a stepping stone to commercial success, marked by the pursuit of contacts that can open doors to new opportunities. However, there's a deeper dimension to networking that transcends the conventional. This article explores the essence of spiritually-aligned networking, a paradigm that intertwines business networking with spiritual values and ethics. It redefines networking as a tool for business advancement and a pathway to forge relationships that resonate with mutual growth, shared values, and profound engagement. We delve into how spiritually-aligned networking is rooted in authenticity, mutual respect, and a commitment to higher purposes, and its transformative impact on both personal and professional spheres.

Redefining Networking with a Spiritual Lens

Traditionally, networking has been viewed through a purely business-focused lens. Spiritually-aligned networking, however, invites us to reimagine this concept.

> **Beyond Transactional Exchanges:** Spiritually-aligned networking seeks connections that go beyond transactional exchanges to foster deeper relationships based on shared values and mutual respect.

> **The Synergy of Values and Business:** This approach aligns one's spiritual and ethical beliefs with their business interactions, ensuring that connections are not just beneficial but also resonate with one's core values.

Authenticity: The Heartbeat of Spiritual Networking

Authenticity is the cornerstone of spiritually-aligned networking. It's about being true to oneself and others in every interaction.

> **Genuine Self-Representation:** Networking with authenticity involves presenting oneself honestly, without exaggerating credentials or skills, and being open about one's values and goals.

> **Seeking Authentic Connections:** It also means seeking out others who are genuine in their intentions and actions, creating a network based on trust and credibility.

Mutual Respect: Fostering Equitable Relationships

Mutual respect is a critical element of spiritually-aligned networking. It acknowledges the value and contributions of each individual in the network.

Respect for Diversity: Embracing diversity in opinions, backgrounds, and experiences and treating each connection with equal regard and appreciation.

Building Equitable Connections: Networking intends to give as much as you receive, fostering mutually beneficial and supportive relationships.

Shared Commitment to Higher Purposes

Spiritually-aligned networking often involves a shared commitment to broader, altruistic goals beyond individual success.

Networking with a Cause: Aligning with individuals and organizations that are committed to causes like sustainability, social justice, or community development.

Impact-Driven Networking: Forming connections that aim to create positive change in the industry or community, transcending personal or organizational gains.

The Importance of Intentionality in Networking

Intentionality is key in spiritually-aligned networking. It's about being purposeful in the connections one makes and nurtures.

Quality Over Quantity: Focusing on the depth and quality of connections rather than the number of contacts in one's network.

Strategic Relationship Building: Mindfully building relationships that align with one's personal and professional growth objectives.

Contributions to Personal and Professional Growth

Spiritually-aligned networking contributes significantly to both personal and professional development.

Personal Development: These connections often lead to personal growth, as they are based on shared values and mutual support.

Professional Advancement: Professionally, they can lead to collaborations and opportunities that are aligned with one's ethical and business goals.

Examples of Spiritually Aligned Networking in Practice

A Business Leader's Ethical Network: A case study of a business leader who built a network centred around sustainable business practices, leading to collaborations that promoted environmental consciousness in the industry.

A Community-Based Networking Initiative: An example of a networking group focused on social entrepreneurship, connecting individuals dedicated to creating social change through business.

Spiritually-aligned networking represents a paradigm shift in how relationships are formed and nurtured in business. It's about building a network that propels one's business forward and aligns with one's deeper spiritual and ethical values. This approach to networking is not merely about accumulating contacts; it's about creating meaningful connections that contribute to personal fulfilment, professional success, and the greater good. Spiritually-aligned networking paves the way for a more conscious, collaborative, and value-driven business landscape by embodying authenticity, mutual respect, and a commitment to higher purposes.

Creating Resonant Connections: The Art of Networking with Shared Values and Vision

In the realm of business, the power of networking is undeniable. However, the true potential of networking is realized when connections are professional and resonate with shared spiritual and ethical values. This article delves into the strategies for identifying and connecting with like-minded individuals and organizations, exploring the avenues to leverage various platforms and events for purposeful networking. It also discusses how effectively communicating one's values and visions can attract the right connections, leading to both professionally advantageous and personally fulfilling relationships.

Understanding the Need for Value-Aligned Networking

The shift from conventional networking to making connections based on shared values represents a significant change in the business landscape.

> **The Rise of Purpose-Driven Networking:** Exploring the growing trend where professionals seek more than just business opportunities in their networking endeavours – they seek connections that align with their spiritual and ethical values.

> **Benefits of Like-Minded Connections:** Discuss how networking with individuals and organizations that share similar values can lead to more meaningful collaborations, robust support systems, and a greater sense of community.

Strategies for Identifying Like-Minded Professionals

Finding individuals and organizations that resonate with one's values requires a targeted approach.

> **Leveraging Online Platforms:** Utilizing social media, professional networking sites, and online forums dedicated to specific causes or values. These platforms can be goldmines for finding like-minded professionals and groups.

> **Purpose-Driven Events and Conferences:** Attending conferences, seminars, and workshops focused on specific areas of interest, such as sustainability, social entrepreneurship, or ethical business practices, can provide opportunities to connect with individuals who share similar passions.

Effective Communication of Values and Visions

Articulating one's values and visions is crucial in attracting the right connections.

> **Crafting a Compelling Personal Brand:** Developing a personal brand that clearly reflects one's values and visions.

This includes how one presents themselves on professional platforms, in business meetings, and at networking events.

Storytelling and Authentic Engagement: Using storytelling as a tool to share one's journey, values, and vision. Authentic stories can resonate deeply with like-minded individuals, fostering genuine connections.

Participating in Community Events and Initiatives

Community events and initiatives can be a practical way to network with individuals with similar values.

Volunteering and Community Involvement: Participating in volunteer work or community projects related to one's values and interests. This provides networking opportunities and demonstrates one's commitment to their values.

Collaborative Projects and Initiatives: Seeking out or initiating projects that align with one's values, which can serve as a platform for connecting with like-minded professionals.

Navigating Challenges in Value-Aligned Networking

While networking with like-minded individuals has many benefits, it also comes with its set of challenges.

Balancing Professional and Personal Values: Addressing the challenge of balancing one's professional goals with personal values in networking situations.

Avoiding Echo Chambers: Avoid limiting oneself to an echo chamber, where diverse perspectives are not explored or valued.

Networking with shared values and vision transcends the traditional business exchange and builds a community of like-minded professionals. This approach to networking is not just about advancing one's career or business interests; it's about creating a network that supports one's entire being – professionally, spiritually, and ethically. By targeting the right platforms, effectively communicating one's values, and engaging in community events, individuals can build connections that are not only professionally rewarding but also align with their deeper beliefs and visions. This networking form opens avenues for fulfilling and impactful collaborations, creating positive change in the professional world.

Cultivating Depth in Connections: The Journey of Nurturing Long-Term, Meaningful Relationships

In the vast and often transient world of professional networking, the art of nurturing long-term, meaningful relationships stands out as a cornerstone for sustainable personal and business growth. This article delves into the significance and methods of cultivating connections that transcend the realm of professional convenience, evolving into partnerships characterized by trust, mutual support, and shared growth. We explore the nuanced strategies for maintaining meaningful communication, being a dependable support system, and collaboratively working towards common goals. This piece also examines the critical roles of empathy, active listening, and resource sharing in fortifying these relationships.

The Essence of Long-Term Professional Relationships

Building long-lasting relationships in the business world is about creating bonds that are rich in trust and mutual understanding.

> **Beyond Professional Convenience:** These relationships go beyond the immediate exchange of services or information; they are about forming bonds that provide mutual support and growth over time.

> **Foundations of Trust and Mutual Respect:** The bedrock of such relationships is trust and mutual respect, which are cultivated through consistent and honest interactions.

Strategies for Nurturing Lasting Relationships

Maintaining and nurturing professional relationships requires thoughtful and consistent effort.

> **Regular and Meaningful Communication:** Keeping in touch through regular check-ins, updates, and meaningful conversations helps keep the relationship vibrant and relevant.

Being a Reliable Support: Reliability in fulfilling promises and being available for support during critical moments is essential in strengthening these bonds.

Collaborating Towards Shared Goals

Working collaboratively on shared goals or interests can significantly enhance the strength and value of professional relationships.

Identifying Common Goals: Finding common objectives or interests that align with the values and goals of both parties can pave the way for collaborative endeavours.

Joint Projects and Ventures: Engaging in joint projects or business ventures can effectively solidify the relationship and achieve mutual growth.

The Power of Empathy and Active Listening

Empathy and active listening are key skills that enrich professional relationships.

Understanding Perspectives: Empathy allows for a deeper understanding of the other person's perspective, fostering a connection that is empathetic and supportive.

Effective Communication: Active listening ensures that communication is not just a transaction but an exchange of ideas and thoughts that contribute to mutual understanding and respect.

Sharing Knowledge and Resources

Sharing knowledge, expertise, and resources can significantly enhance the value of professional relationships.

Mentorship and Guidance: Offering mentorship or guidance based on one's experience and knowledge can be a powerful way to support and nurture the relationship.

Resource Exchange: Sharing resources, be it contacts, skills, or information, can help both parties grow and succeed in their respective endeavours.

The journey of nurturing long-term, meaningful relationships in a professional setting is about creating a network of trust, support, and shared growth. It's about seeing beyond the immediate benefits of networking and investing in relationships that offer depth and enduring value. Through consistent communication, empathy, collaboration, and resource sharing, these relationships can evolve into partnerships that support business growth and contribute to personal fulfilment and collective success. In a world where professional networks are often transient, nurturing long-term relationships is a testament to genuine connections' enduring power.

Spiritual Networking: Catalyzing Change Beyond Business Boundaries

In today's interconnected world, the power of networking extends well beyond the confines of traditional business. When imbued with spiritual alignment and purpose-driven goals, networking transforms into a potent tool for broad societal impact. This article delves into the far-reaching effects of spiritually-aligned networking, demonstrating how it can amplify influence in the business realm and create positive change in communities and industries. Through a series of case studies and anecdotes, we will explore how purpose-driven networks have catalyzed significant social and environmental impacts, fostering innovation, advocacy, and transformative projects. This exploration will shed light on the powerful role that spiritually-aligned networking plays in driving societal change.

The Transformative Power of Spiritually-Aligned Networking

Spiritually-aligned networking is about connecting with a purpose, transcending personal or organizational gains. It's a form of networking that is deeply rooted in shared values and a commitment to making a positive impact.

> **Beyond Professional Networking:** This approach to networking goes beyond the traditional business objectives of profit and growth, focusing instead on creating meaningful change in society and various industries.

> **Shared Values as the Cornerstone:** The foundation of spiritually-aligned networking is built on shared spiritual and ethical values guiding the actions and collaborations within these networks.

Amplifying Influence in the Business World

Purpose-driven networks have the potential to significantly amplify the influence of their members in the business world.

Expanded Reach and Impact By connecting with like-minded individuals and organizations, members of spiritually-aligned networks can extend their reach and impact, influencing broader industry practices and norms.

Enhanced Credibility and Trust: Networks founded on shared values often enjoy enhanced credibility and trust within their industries and the broader business community.

Contributing to a Greater Cause

One of the most significant aspects of spiritually-aligned networking is its contribution to causes that extend beyond the immediate interests of the network's members.

Social and Environmental Advocacy: Many spiritually-aligned networks actively advocate for social and environmental causes, leveraging their collective influence to drive change.

Support for Community Initiatives: These networks often support community-based initiatives, contributing to local development and well-being.

Creating a Ripple Effect of Positive Change

Spiritually-aligned networking often creates a ripple effect, leading to positive changes that extend far beyond the original network.

Influence on Industry Practices: Networks can influence industry practices by setting new standards in ethical business, sustainability, or social responsibility.

Inspiring Others to Follow: The success of these networks can inspire other businesses and organizations to adopt similar values and practices, amplifying the overall impact.

Spiritually-aligned networking represents a paradigm shift in forming and leveraging professional relationships. It's about harnessing the collective power of like-minded individuals and organizations to achieve business success and drive meaningful change. Through shared values, advocacy, and collaborative initiatives, these networks demonstrate the immense potential of networking when aligned with a higher purpose. The case studies and examples highlighted here illustrate the profound impact that spiritually-aligned networking can have within the business community and in shaping a more sustainable, equitable, and compassionate world.

Ch 11. Marketing with Heart: Authentic and value-driven marketing strategies

In a world where consumers increasingly seek meaning and connection, this chapter offers a refreshing and much-needed perspective on how businesses can resonate deeply with their audiences. This chapter is a deep dive into marketing, reimagined through the lenses of authenticity, ethical practices, and value-driven strategies. It transcends the conventional approach of persuasive advertising to embrace a more heartfelt, empathetic, and genuine way of connecting with customers.

At the heart of this new marketing paradigm lies the belief that businesses can and should be forces for good, aligning their marketing strategies with their core values and customers' needs.

Building Authentic Brand Narratives

Authenticity is the cornerstone of heart-centered marketing. It's about crafting brand stories that are compelling and true reflections of what the business stands for. Storytelling can be leveraged to communicate a brand's journey, its commitment to certain values, and the impact it aims to create.

Creating Value-Based Content

Content is a crucial element in this approach to marketing, but it goes beyond traditional advertising to content rich in values and purpose.

Ethics and Empathy in Marketing Practices

In heart-centred marketing, ethical considerations and empathy are not just add-ons but integral parts of the marketing strategy.

The Ripple Effect of Value-Driven Marketing

Heart-centered marketing is not just beneficial for the business and its customers; it has a broader impact, creating a ripple effect of positive change.

As we navigate this chapter, we'll discover that marketing with heart is not just about promoting a product or service; it's about building a movement, a community, and a legacy. It's about businesses taking a stand, sharing their journey, and inviting customers to be a part of something bigger. This approach to marketing is a powerful tool for businesses to achieve commercial success and make a meaningful impact on the world. Through this exploration, we'll see how aligning a company's marketing strategies with its core values can create a resonant and influential brand voice that truly speaks to the hearts of its audience.

Embracing Authenticity: The Transformative Journey of Heart-Centered Marketing

In the contemporary business landscape, the traditional marketing approach is undergoing a significant transformation. The emerging philosophy of heart-centered marketing steers away from aggressive sales tactics and towards a more empathetic, authentic, and value-driven approach. This article delves into the foundational principles of heart-centred marketing, highlighting its focus on authenticity, empathy, and ethical values. We explore the transition from conventional marketing methods to strategies that resonate deeply with the business's and customers' core values and beliefs. This journey into heart-centred marketing also examines how this philosophy aligns with the mission and vision of spiritually conscious companies, emphasizing the crucial roles of trust, transparency, and genuine connection in all marketing communications.

The Shift to Heart-Centered Marketing

The transition to heart-centred marketing represents a profound change in how businesses approach customer relationships.

From Selling to Connecting: Traditional marketing often focuses on persuading customers to buy. In contrast, heart-centered marketing is about forming a genuine connection with the audience, understanding their needs and values, and reflecting these in the marketing efforts.

Building Relationships over Transactions: This approach prioritizes long-term relationships over one-time transactions. It's about creating a bond with the customer that is based on mutual understanding and respect.

The philosophy of heart-centered marketing is built upon several key pillars.

Authenticity in Communication: Authenticity is at the heart of this approach. It involves being truthful and honest in marketing messages, avoiding exaggeration, and genuinely presenting the brand and its offerings.

Empathy with the Audience: Empathy allows businesses to understand and connect with their audience truly. It involves putting oneself in the customers' shoes and addressing their needs and concerns through marketing efforts.

Upholding Ethical Values: Ethical values are non-negotiable in heart-centered marketing. This means respecting the customer, being transparent about products and services, and avoiding misleading information.

Aligning with the Spiritual Consciousness of Business

Heart-centred marketing is particularly resonant with businesses with a spiritual or ethical focus.

Reflecting the Business's Spiritual Mission: Marketing strategies are designed to reflect the business's spiritual mission, ensuring that every message and campaign aligns with the company's core values.

Promoting a Vision of Social and Environmental Responsibility: This approach often involves promoting the business's commitment to social and environmental responsibility, resonating with customers who share similar values.

Building Trust and Transparency

Trust and transparency are critical components of heart-centered marketing.

Earning Customer Trust: Trust is earned by consistently being honest and transparent in all marketing communications. This includes being open about the business practices, product ingredients, or service processes.

Transparent Practices: Transparency in business practices, such as sourcing materials, manufacturing processes, or pricing, strengthens customer trust and loyalty.

Heart-centered marketing represents a paradigm shift in the business world. It's a move towards more human, empathetic, and value-driven approaches to connecting with customers. This philosophy aligns with the mission and vision of spiritually conscious businesses and builds a foundation of trust and genuine connection with the audience. By embracing this approach, businesses can forge stronger, more meaningful relationships with their customers, leading to lasting loyalty and shared success. Through examples and an in-depth exploration of its principles, it becomes clear that heart-centered marketing is not just a strategy but a holistic way of conducting business with integrity and purpose.

Narratives That Resonate: Crafting Authentic Brand Stories

In the realm of modern marketing, the art of storytelling has emerged as a pivotal tool for businesses to connect with their audiences. However, the most impactful narratives are deeply authentic, echoing a company's ethos, mission, and intrinsic values. This article delves into the critical importance of crafting authentic brand narratives that go beyond mere storytelling to genuinely reflect a company's identity and the value it brings to its customers' lives. We explore various techniques for developing these narratives, emphasizing the roles of honesty and vulnerability in making brand stories not just compelling but also relatable and powerful.

The Power of Authentic Brand Narratives

Authentic brand narratives are more than just marketing tools; they are the heart and soul of a company's communication with its audience.

Beyond the Surface: Authentic brand stories delve deeper than traditional marketing narratives, reflecting the true essence of the brand's identity, mission, and values.

Creating Emotional Connections: A well-crafted, authentic narrative can create an emotional connection with the audience, making the brand more relatable and memorable.

Developing Authentic Brand Narratives

Developing these narratives involves various steps, each focused on showcasing the genuine character of the brand.

Reflecting the Company's Journey: Start by sharing the company's journey, including its origins, challenges, triumphs, and evolution. This helps build a narrative that is engaging and offers insight into the company's core ethos.

Showcasing Commitments: Highlight the company's commitment to social and environmental causes, and how these commitments are woven into the fabric of its operations and ethos.

Illustrating Tangible Impact: Include stories or examples that illustrate the tangible impact that the company has made in its field, community, or on environmental causes.

The Role of Honesty and Vulnerability

Honesty and vulnerability play crucial roles in crafting these narratives in enhancing their authenticity and relatability.

Embracing Honesty: Be honest in the narrative, even if it involves acknowledging past mistakes or learning curves. This honesty resonates with audiences, as it reflects the brand's genuineness.

Vulnerability as a Strength: Showing vulnerability, such as discussing challenges or uncertainties faced, can strengthen the connection with the audience, as it portrays the brand as relatable and trustworthy.

Techniques for Crafting Authentic Narratives

Several techniques can be employed to ensure the narratives are authentically aligned with the brand's identity and mission.

Storytelling with Purpose: Each story should have a clear purpose: to inspire, educate, or reflect the brand's values.

Incorporating Real Stories: Use real stories from within the company, customer testimonials, or case studies to add depth and authenticity to the narrative.

Authentic brand narratives represent a powerful means for companies to communicate their essence. Beyond mere marketing, these narratives are the true stories that define the brand, resonate with audiences, and build lasting connections. By focusing on honesty, vulnerability, and real impact, these narratives become stories that testify to the brand's commitment to its values and mission. Through real-world examples and in-depth exploration, we see how these authentic narratives can powerfully influence both brand perception and customer engagement, paving the way for more meaningful and impactful brand relationships.

Content with a Conscience: Bridging Values and Vision in Customer Engagement

In an era where content is king, the challenge for many businesses is not just to create content that captivates and informs but also to produce material that resonates with the core values of both the company and its audience. This article delves into the intricate process of creating value-based content, which serves a purpose far beyond mere product promotion. It's about developing content that educates, inspires, and fosters a deep connection with the audience, aligning with their interests and values such as sustainability, wellness, or community development. We explore various content formats, from blogs and social media posts to webinars and podcasts, and examine how they can effectively create a sense of community and shared purpose.

The Rise of Value-Based Content

In the current digital landscape, content has become a primary communication medium between businesses and their customers.

Beyond Informative and Engaging: Today's consumers seek content that goes beyond being merely informative or entertaining. They are drawn to content that mirrors their values and beliefs.

Aligning with Audience Values: The key to effective content creation lies in understanding and aligning with the values and interests of the target audience.

Crafting Content That Reflects Shared Values

Creating content that reflects shared values requires a deep understanding of both the company's ethos and the audience's preferences.

Research and Understanding: Deep research into the audience's values, interests, and preferences is crucial. This includes understanding their concerns about issues like sustainability, wellness, or social responsibility.

Incorporating Company Values: The company's values should be seamlessly woven into the content. For instance, if a business stands for environmental sustainability, this should be a consistent theme across its content.

Diverse Formats to Engage and Inspire

The diversity of content formats available today offers numerous ways to engage with audiences effectively.

Blogs and Articles: Blogs and articles provide a platform for in-depth exploration of topics that matter to the audience, allowing for storytelling that can educate and inspire.

Social Media Posts: Social media offers a more immediate and interactive way to engage with audiences, using shorter, more dynamic content.

Webinars and Podcasts: These formats allow for deeper engagement, often bringing in experts to discuss relevant topics, which can be particularly effective for topics like wellness and community development.

Strategies for Developing Value-Based Content

Developing content that resonates with the audience's values involves several strategic considerations.

Authenticity and Relevance: Content must be authentic and relevant to the audience. This means avoiding overly promotional material and focusing on providing real value.

Storytelling and Emotional Connection: Using storytelling to connect emotionally with the audience can be powerful. This could include customer stories, behind-the-scenes looks at the company, or stories about how the company's products or services are making a difference.

Fostering a Sense of Community and Shared Purpose

Value-based content can foster a sense of community and shared purpose among the audience.

Creating Community Platforms: Encouraging discussions and interactions among audience members through forums or social media groups can help build a community around shared value.

Collaborative Initiatives: Inviting the audience to participate in collaborative initiatives, such as social responsibility projects or environmental campaigns, can deepen the sense of community and shared purpose.

Real-World Examples of Value-Based Content

A Sustainable Brand's Storytelling: An example of a sustainable brand that uses its blog and social media to share stories about its sustainable practices and the impact of these practices on the environment.

A Wellness Company's Podcast Series: A wellness company that runs a podcast series featuring experts in health and wellness, providing valuable information to its audience while aligning with its core values of promoting health and wellbeing.

Value-based content represents a strategic shift in how businesses communicate with their audience. It's about crafting content that informs and, entertains and embodies the shared values and beliefs of the company and its customers. Businesses can create deeper, more meaningful connections with their customers by aligning content with these shared values and utilizing diverse formats to engage the audience. This approach enhances customer loyalty and fosters a sense of community and shared purpose, ultimately contributing to a more engaged and responsive audience base.

Integrity in Interaction: The Ethical and Empathetic Approach to Marketing

In the dynamic world of marketing, where persuasion and influence are the tools of the trade, ethical and empathetic practices often take a backseat. However, there is a growing recognition of the importance of integrating ethical considerations and empathy into marketing strategies. This article delves into the realm of ethical and empathetic marketing practices, emphasizing the significance of honesty in advertising, respect for customer privacy, and the avoidance of manipulative tactics. It provides an in-depth analysis of developing marketing campaigns that honor the intelligence and values of the audience, adhere to ethical advertising standards, embrace consent-based marketing, and genuinely strive to improve customers' lives or address their concerns.

The Foundation of Ethical Marketing

Ethical marketing is built on the principles of honesty, transparency, and respect for the consumer.

> **Honesty in Advertising:** The importance of truthfulness in advertising cannot be overstated. This means avoiding misleading information, exaggerated claims, or deceptive visuals that could misguide the consumer.

> **Transparency in Communication:** Transparency involves openly sharing information about products or services, including any potential drawbacks or limitations.

Respecting Customer Privacy

In an age where data is king, respecting customer privacy has become a cornerstone of ethical marketing.

> **Consent-Based Data Usage:** This involves obtaining explicit consent from customers before collecting or using their data, ensuring their privacy is not infringed upon.

> **Data Protection and Security:** Protecting customer data against unauthorized access or breaches is critical to respecting customer privacy.

Empathy in Understanding Customer Needs

Empathy plays a crucial role in understanding and addressing customer needs and concerns.

Listening to the Customer: This involves actively listening to customer feedback and concerns and using this information to guide marketing strategies.

Addressing Real Needs: Empathetic marketing focuses on addressing the real needs and concerns of the customer rather than creating a perceived need.

Developing Ethical Marketing Campaigns

Creating marketing campaigns that are both effective and ethical involves several key considerations.

Value-Driven Campaigns: Campaigns should be driven by the values of the brand and the audience, ensuring that they resonate on a deeper level.

Avoiding Manipulative Tactics: This includes steering clear of tactics that exploit consumer vulnerabilities, such as fear or insecurity.

Ethical Advertising Standards

Adhering to ethical advertising standards is essential in maintaining the trust and loyalty of consumers.

Industry Guidelines and Regulations: Familiarity with and adherence to industry guidelines and regulations is crucial in ensuring that marketing practices are ethical.

Self-Regulation: Beyond legal requirements, companies should embrace self-regulation to ensure that their marketing practices align with their ethical standards.

Consent-Based Marketing

Consent-based marketing respects the customer's choice and autonomy in receiving marketing communications.

Opt-In and Opt-Out Options: Providing clear opt-in and opt-out options for marketing communications is a fundamental aspect of consent-based marketing.

> **Personalization with Permission:** Personalizing marketing communications should be done with the customer's explicit permission.

Marketing Campaigns That Improve Lives

The ultimate goal of ethical and empathetic marketing should be to create campaigns that genuinely seek to improve the lives of customers.

> **Beneficial Products and Services:** Focusing on products and services that offer real benefits to the customer rather than creating a false sense of need.

> **Addressing Customer Concerns:** Campaigns should address customer concerns or challenges, providing solutions that make a tangible difference in their lives.

Ethical and empathetic marketing represents a paradigm shift from traditional practices, focusing on building trust, transparency, and a genuine connection with the audience. By embracing these principles, businesses can develop marketing strategies that resonate with their customers and contribute positively to their lives. This approach fosters customer loyalty and satisfaction and enhances the brand's reputation as a trustworthy and responsible entity in the marketplace.

Ch 12. Giving Back: Philanthropy and community engagement as a spiritual practice

In the landscape of modern business, where the pursuit of success often dominates the narrative, a profound and transformative approach is emerging: giving back through philanthropy and community engagement as a form of spiritual practice. More than a mere corporate responsibility or a strategic public relations exercise, this concept embodies a deeper, more holistic understanding of a business's role in society. It's an approach where philanthropy and community engagement transcend their traditional boundaries to become integral elements of a company's spiritual DNA.

At the heart of this philosophy lies the recognition that a business's impact extends far beyond the products it creates or the services it provides. There is a growing awareness among business leaders that their organizations have the power – and perhaps the responsibility – to contribute positively to the societal and environmental fabric of our world. This realization is leading to a redefinition of corporate success, one that values not just financial profitability but also the well-being of communities and the nurturing of human connections.

Philanthropy, in this context, is reimagined. It's no longer seen just as a means of financial giving but as a way to forge meaningful relationships with the community and the environment. It becomes an expression of a company's core values and beliefs, a tangible manifestation of its commitment to a greater good. When a business aligns its philanthropic endeavours with its mission and values, it does more than just provide aid; it creates a powerful narrative of care, empathy, and connectedness.

Similarly, community engagement takes on a new dimension as a spiritual practice. It's about actively participating in the betterment of society, not just through financial contributions but through actions that reflect a deep understanding of and commitment to the community's needs. It's about building bridges, fostering a spirit of collaboration, and empowering communities. Such engagement allows businesses and their employees to connect with people and causes in a way that enriches both their own lives and those of others.

Moreover, this approach to giving back is becoming an essential component of a business's identity. Consumers and employees alike are increasingly drawn to organizations that demonstrate a genuine commitment to social and environmental causes. In this sense, philanthropy and community engagement are not just good for the world; they're good for business, too. They help build trust and loyalty among customers, attract and retain talented employees who are looking for purpose in their work, and create a positive brand image.

As we delve deeper into the topic of "Giving Back: Philanthropy and Community Engagement as Spiritual Practice," we will explore how businesses are incorporating these concepts into their operations, the impact of these actions on the companies and the communities they serve, and the spiritual fulfilment that comes from this form of corporate generosity. We will see that when businesses approach philanthropy and community engagement as aspects of their spiritual practice, they can effect profound and lasting change – not just in the communities they serve but within their organizations as well.

The Spiritual Foundations of Philanthropy in Business

In the ever-evolving narrative of modern business, the concept of philanthropy has gradually transcended its traditional charitable connotations, rooting itself deeply in the spiritual and philosophical foundations of corporate ethos. This shift has seen businesses not just engaging in philanthropy for philanthropy's sake, but as a genuine reflection of their core spiritual values. The infusion of compassion, empathy, and a profound sense of interconnectedness with the community into business practices marks a significant shift in how companies perceive their role and impact in society.

The spiritual underpinnings of philanthropy in business are diverse and multifaceted, drawing from various traditions and philosophies that have long emphasized the importance of altruism and giving back. These principles, deeply ingrained in human culture, have provided a moral and ethical framework that many businesses are now embracing. The integration of these principles into corporate culture signifies a shift towards a more holistic, value-driven approach to business success, where financial profitability coexists with social and environmental responsibility.

One key aspect of this transformation is the recognition of the interconnectedness of all life, a concept central to many spiritual traditions. This view holds that every action, no matter how small, has a ripple effect, impacting the wider community and, by extension, the world. For businesses, this means that their operations, products, and services are not isolated from the society and environment they operate in. Therefore, philanthropy becomes a way for businesses to acknowledge and act upon this interconnectedness, to contribute positively to the societal fabric that sustains them.

Another fundamental aspect of the spiritual foundation of philanthropy in business is the concept of compassion. Rooted in the understanding of shared human experience and suffering, compassion drives businesses to look beyond their corporate interests and consider the well-being of the community. This empathetic approach often leads to initiatives aimed at alleviating social issues, enhancing community welfare, and generally improving the quality of life for those less fortunate.

Furthermore, the principle of empathy extends beyond compassion, urging businesses to not only acknowledge the struggles of others but to actively feel with them. This deep sense of empathy can be a powerful motivator for philanthropic activities, pushing companies to engage in more meaningful and impactful ways with the communities they serve. Empathy in business philanthropy fosters a culture of care, understanding, and genuine concern, which in turn nurtures a more loyal and engaged customer base, as well as a more committed and satisfied workforce.

Ethical frameworks from various spiritual traditions also play a crucial role in shaping the philanthropic endeavours of businesses. These frameworks provide a moral compass, guiding companies in their quest to do good in the world. Principles such as honesty, integrity, and fairness are not just lofty ideals in these frameworks but are essential components of a business's operations and philanthropic activities. By adhering to these ethical principles, businesses ensure that their philanthropic efforts are not only effective but also just and equitable.

Different spiritual traditions offer unique perspectives on the role of altruism and giving back. For instance, many Eastern philosophies, such as Buddhism and Hinduism, emphasize the concept of karma – the idea that good deeds lead to positive outcomes. This belief can inspire businesses to engage in philanthropy as a way of creating positive karmic effects, both for the company and the wider community. In Western traditions, such as Christianity, Judaism, and Islam, the concept of charity is deeply ingrained, viewed as both a moral duty and a path to spiritual fulfilment. These traditions encourage businesses to view philanthropy as an integral part of their spiritual journey, a means of giving back to the community that sustains them.

Integrating these spiritual and ethical principles into a business's ethos requires a deliberate and thoughtful approach. It involves redefining the company's mission and values to reflect a commitment to social and environmental responsibility. It also means embedding these principles into every aspect of the business, from decision-making processes to day-to-day operations. This integration results in a business model that not only seeks financial success but also strives to make a positive impact on the world.

The contribution of these spiritual principles to holistic business success is significant. Companies that embrace this approach often find that it leads to more sustainable and long-lasting success. They build stronger relationships with their customers and communities, fostering trust and loyalty. Their employees are often more motivated and engaged, knowing that their work contributes to a greater good. Furthermore, these companies often enjoy a positive public image, enhancing their reputation and standing in the marketplace.

The spiritual foundations of philanthropy in business represent a profound and meaningful approach to corporate social responsibility. By drawing on various spiritual and ethical traditions, businesses can develop a more compassionate, empathetic, and interconnected way of operating. This approach not only benefits the communities and environments in which these businesses operate but also contributes to a more fulfilling and sustainable form of business success. As more companies embrace these spiritual principles, we may see a shift towards a more compassionate and responsible business world, where success is measured not just in financial terms, but in terms of the positive impact on society and the planet.

Harmonizing Giving with Values: Crafting a Philanthropic Strategy That Echoes Corporate Ethos

In the contemporary corporate world, philanthropy has evolved beyond mere charitable giving to become a strategic component deeply aligned with a company's core values and spiritual beliefs. This evolution calls for a nuanced approach to developing a philanthropic strategy that resonates with a company's mission, embodies its ethical convictions, and reflects its commitment to making a meaningful impact. This article delves into the practical aspects of creating and implementing such a philanthropic strategy, focusing on aligning philanthropic activities with the company's ethos, involving employees in these initiatives, and enhancing the spiritual and communal fabric of the workplace.

The process of developing a philanthropic strategy begins with a deep introspection into what a company stands for - its core values, mission, and the beliefs that define its corporate identity. The goal is to ensure that philanthropic activities are not just an addendum to business operations but an authentic expression of the company's inherent values.

Identifying Causes and Initiatives

The first step in aligning philanthropy with corporate values is identifying causes and initiatives that resonate with the company's mission. This involves a careful examination of various social, environmental, and community issues and discerning which among these align most closely with the company's ethos.

For a company deeply rooted in environmental sustainability, for instance, aligning with causes focused on environmental conservation or renewable energy initiatives would be a natural fit. Similarly, a business built on the principles of education and empowerment might find synergy in supporting literacy programs or vocational training for underprivileged communities.

Setting Achievable Goals

Once causes and initiatives have been identified, the next step is setting achievable and meaningful goals. These goals should be specific, measurable, and aligned with the intended impact of the philanthropic efforts. For example, rather than a vague intention to 'support environmental causes,' a more tangible goal would be 'to contribute to the planting of 10,000 trees annually.'

Setting such clear goals not only provides a direction for philanthropic efforts but also helps in measuring the impact of these initiatives, ensuring that they are making a real difference in the areas they intend to serve.

Measuring Impact

Measuring the impact of philanthropic efforts is crucial in understanding their effectiveness and in making necessary adjustments to ensure that these initiatives continue to align with the company's values and desired outcomes. Impact measurement can take various forms, from assessing the direct outcomes of the initiatives, like the number of trees planted or the number of students who benefitted from a scholarship program, to evaluating the long-term effects on the community or the environment.

Employee Involvement in Philanthropy

Involving employees in philanthropic initiatives is a powerful way to enhance the spiritual and communal aspects of the workplace. When employees engage in activities that resonate with their personal values and beliefs, it fosters a sense of purpose and fulfilment that transcends the routine of their daily work.

Employee involvement can take many forms, from volunteering in community service programs to participating in decision-making processes related to the company's philanthropic activities. Such involvement not only deepens the employees' connection with the company's mission but also encourages a culture of generosity and empathy within the workplace.

Authenticity in Philanthropic Efforts

Ensuring authenticity in philanthropic efforts is essential. This means that the initiatives should genuinely reflect the company's values and should not be driven by the desire for public recognition or business benefits alone. Authentic philanthropy is about making a real difference, about genuinely caring for the causes the company stands for, and about being committed to positive change.

Enhancing the Spiritual Fabric of the Company

Philanthropy, when aligned with a company's core values and spiritual beliefs, can significantly enhance the spiritual fabric of the company. It allows the company to not just exist as a commercial entity but to operate as a community of individuals united by a shared commitment to certain values and causes. This communal aspect of philanthropy can be deeply enriching, creating a workplace environment that is not just productive but also spiritually fulfilling.

Developing a philanthropic strategy that is aligned with a company's core values and spiritual beliefs is a complex yet profoundly rewarding endeavor. It requires a thoughtful approach, one that involves careful selection of causes, setting of meaningful goals, authentic engagement, and active employee involvement. Such a strategy not only contributes to societal and environmental wellbeing but also nurtures the spiritual and communal dimensions of the workplace, creating a corporate culture that is as compassionate as it is successful.

Cultivating Community, Nurturing Spirit: The Transformative Power of Community Engagement

In the contemporary business world, where the relentless pursuit of profit often overshadows deeper values, the concept of community engagement emerges as a beacon of hope and spirituality. More than just a corporate social responsibility initiative, community engagement, when approached as a form of spiritual practice, has the potential to profoundly deepen a company's spiritual journey, forge meaningful connections, and leave a lasting impact on both the community and the corporation. This exploration into community engagement as a spiritual practice will illuminate the various forms it can take, from volunteerism to partnerships with local organizations, and delve into the multitude of benefits these activities offer for spiritual growth, community well-being, and the cultivation of a sense of belonging and purpose among employees.

The essence of community engagement as a spiritual practice lies in its ability to transcend the traditional boundaries of business operations and enter a realm where corporate actions align with deeper, more humane values. This alignment opens doors to experiences that not only benefit external communities but also enrich the internal corporate culture, fostering a spirit of togetherness, empathy, and mutual growth.

Forms of Community Engagement

Community engagement can manifest in numerous forms, each offering unique pathways for companies to contribute meaningfully to society while nurturing their own spiritual core.

Volunteerism: One of the most direct forms of community engagement, volunteerism involves employees actively participating in community service projects. This could range from helping in local shelters, participating in environmental clean-ups, to mentoring programs for underprivileged youth. Such hands-on involvement allows employees to experience the immediate impact of their efforts, fostering a sense of accomplishment and connection with the community.

Partnerships with Local Organizations: By partnering with local nonprofits or community groups, companies can contribute resources, expertise, or financial support to ongoing community initiatives. These partnerships often lead to more structured and sustained community engagement efforts, allowing companies to be part of larger, long-term projects that align with their core values and mission.

Community Development Programs: Companies can initiate or support community development programs that address specific local needs. This could include initiatives like building community centers, supporting local arts and culture, or developing educational programs. By contributing to the development of the community, companies can help create a more vibrant, healthy, and sustainable environment for both residents and their own employees.

Benefits of Community Engagement

The benefits of community engagement extend far beyond the tangible outcomes of the initiatives themselves.

Spiritual Growth and Fulfilment: Engaging in community service provides a profound sense of spiritual fulfilment. It offers an opportunity for employees and the company as a whole to reflect on their broader purpose, to connect with values like compassion, altruism, and service, and to experience the joy and satisfaction that comes from helping others.

Strengthening Community Ties: Active involvement in community initiatives helps build stronger ties between the company and the local community. It demonstrates a commitment to the well-being of the society in which the business operates, fostering goodwill and a positive reputation.

Employee Engagement and Morale: Community engagement initiatives can significantly boost employee morale and engagement. Participating in such activities can break the monotony of the daily work routine, provide opportunities for team building, and instill a sense of pride and belonging among employees.

Fostering a Sense of Belonging and Purpose: Involvement in community activities can foster a deep sense of belonging and purpose, both at an individual and corporate level. It helps employees see themselves as part of something larger than their job or the company itself, as contributors to the well-being of their community and society at large.

Community Engagement in Action: Case Studies

Illustrative examples of successful community engagement initiatives can provide valuable insights into how these practices can be effectively implemented and the impacts they can have.

A Corporation's Long-Term Partnership with a Local Charity: A case study of a corporation that established a long-term partnership with a local charity, detailing the initiatives they undertook together, the impacts on the community, and the spiritual and cultural changes observed within the corporation.

A Company-Wide Volunteer Day: The story of a company that organized a large-scale volunteer day for its employees, the activities they participated in, and the feedback from employees on how this experience affected their perspectives and sense of belonging within the company.

When embraced as a form of spiritual practice, community engagement can be transformative for both the company and the community. It goes beyond philanthropy or corporate social responsibility, becoming a means of spiritual enrichment, community development, and employee engagement. By actively participating in community initiatives, companies can deepen their spiritual journey, create lasting impacts in the community, and foster a sense of belonging and purpose among their employees. This approach contributes to the societal good and nurtures a corporate culture that values compassion, empathy, and connectedness — essential qualities for any business aspiring to make a positive and lasting mark in the world.

Part V: Personal Growth and Business Evolution

Ch 13. Balancing Business and Spiritual Practice: Strategies for personal well-being

In today's fast-paced and often high-stress business environment, the quest for personal well-being can seem like a daunting, sometimes unreachable goal. Pursuing success, marked by relentless work schedules and constant connectivity, often leaves little room for personal growth and spiritual nourishment. However, the burgeoning recognition of the importance of spiritual well-being in the business world has led to a paradigm shift. This chapter explores this new terrain, where harmonising business acumen with spiritual practice is possible but essential for sustainable success and personal fulfilment.

The premise of this chapter is founded on the understanding that the well-being of an individual is not merely a function of physical health or financial success, but also of spiritual fulfilment and mental peace. It acknowledges business professionals' challenges in maintaining this balance and offers strategies to integrate spiritual practices into their daily business routines. This integration is not about compromising business efficiency or productivity; rather, it's about enhancing these aspects through a more centred, mindful, and holistic approach to both life and work.

One of the key areas explored in this chapter is the integration of mindfulness into the daily business routine. Mindfulness, the practice of being fully present and engaged in the moment, has been shown to have profound benefits on mental clarity, stress reduction, and decision-making. This section of the chapter will delve into how simple yet effective mindfulness techniques can be seamlessly woven into the fabric of the business day, from mindful breathing exercises during breaks to being fully present in meetings and business interactions. The emphasis here is on the practicality of these practices, ensuring they are accessible and feasible for busy professionals.

Another significant aspect covered in this chapter is achieving a work-life balance in a high-pressure environment. Work-life balance is often touted as a key ingredient for personal well-being, yet it remains elusive for many in the corporate world. This section will address the common hurdles in achieving this balance and offer tangible strategies, such as setting boundaries, prioritizing tasks, and ensuring quality downtime. The focus will be on practical steps individuals can take to ensure their professional lives do not overwhelm their time and space.

Further, the chapter delves into cultivating spiritual growth within the workplace. It posits that personal values and spiritual beliefs need not be left at the office door but can be integrated into one's professional life. This integration not only adds a layer of fulfilment to the work but also brings a sense of purpose and integrity to one's professional role. This section will also explore creating a workplace environment that supports spiritual growth, including respecting diverse beliefs and practices among colleagues.

Lastly, the chapter addresses the development of spiritual resilience to navigate business challenges effectively. In the unpredictable and often tumultuous world of business, resilience is key. This section will explore how spiritual practices and perspectives can provide strength and guidance during challenging times. It will cover topics such as dealing with failure, handling uncertainty, and maintaining a positive outlook in adversity.

In essence, this chapter is about finding harmony between two worlds often seen as separate – the world of business and spiritual practice. It acknowledges that for many professionals, work is an integral part of their identity and life. Therefore, including spiritual practices in business is beneficial and necessary for a well-rounded, fulfilling life. Through thoughtful insights, practical strategies, and real-life examples, this chapter aims to guide readers on a journey to achieving personal well-being amidst the demands of their professional lives. It is an invitation to embrace a more holistic approach to success that values mental peace and spiritual growth as much as it does financial gain and professional achievements.

Mindful Mastery: Transforming Business with the Power of Presence

In the dynamic and often tumultuous world of modern business, the pursuit of success is frequently marred by the pressures and stress of the fast-paced environment. Amidst the whirlwind of meetings, deadlines, and decisions, the quest for clarity and calm can seem like a distant dream. However, the ancient practice of mindfulness offers a beacon of hope, a way to navigate the choppy waters of the corporate world with steadiness and composure. This exploration into integrating mindfulness into the daily business routine delves into practical techniques and their transformative effects, focusing on how mindful breathing, meditation, and conscious presence can revolutionize decision-making processes, reduce stress, and enhance overall well-being in the workplace.

Mindfulness, rooted in Buddhist traditions, is the practice of being fully present and engaged at the moment, aware of one's thoughts and feelings without distraction or judgment. In recent years, mindfulness has transcended its spiritual origins to become a vital tool in the corporate arsenal, recognized for enhancing focus, improving mental clarity, and fostering emotional intelligence. By integrating mindfulness practices into the business routine, professionals can cultivate a heightened awareness, enabling them to navigate the complexities of their work with greater ease and effectiveness.

The first step in this integration is the adoption of mindful breathing techniques. Focusing on one's breath is an anchor to the present moment, cutting through the noise and chaos of a busy workday. Conscious breathing can be practised anywhere and at any time – before a crucial meeting, during a challenging task, or during a busy day. This practice helps calm the mind, reduce anxiety, and restore focus, enhancing one's ability to tackle business challenges with a clear and composed mind.

Another powerful mindfulness technique is meditation. While meditating may seem daunting or out of place in a business setting, the practice can be adapted to fit into the corporate lifestyle. Short, guided meditations can profoundly affect one's mental state, even for just a few minutes a day. Meditation sessions can be incorporated into the daily schedule, perhaps at the start of the day, during lunch breaks, or in between meetings. These sessions serve as a reset button, clearing the mind of clutter and sharpening focus, ultimately improving productivity and creativity.

Conscious presence in meetings and decision-making processes is another critical aspect of integrating mindfulness into business. It involves being fully present in interactions and discussions, actively listening, and being cognizant of one's thoughts and responses. This practice fosters a more thoughtful and deliberate approach to communication and decision-making. It encourages a deeper understanding of the matters and leads to more considered and effective decisions. By being mindfully present, professionals can better navigate complex negotiations, resolve conflicts more effectively, and lead with greater empathy and understanding.

The benefits of integrating mindfulness into the business routine extend beyond the individual to impact the broader workplace environment. A culture of mindfulness promotes a more harmonious and supportive work atmosphere. It encourages open communication, enhances teamwork, and fosters a sense of collective well-being. Employees who practice mindfulness are typically more resilient, adaptable, and emotionally intelligent – invaluable qualities in the ever-changing business landscape.

In implementing these mindfulness practices, it is crucial to approach them with consistency and sincerity. Mindfulness is not a quick fix or a one-time solution; it is a continuous practice that requires dedication and commitment. Businesses serious about integrating mindfulness into their routine should consider offering employees training sessions, workshops, or resources. This equips the workforce with valuable tools and signals a commitment to their overall well-being and professional development.

Hence, integrating mindfulness into the business routine offers a pathway to a more centred, clear, and productive work life. It equips professionals with the tools to navigate the complexities and pressures of the business world with grace and effectiveness. Through mindful breathing, meditation, and conscious presence, individuals can transform their work experience, leading to better decision-making and reduced stress and a more fulfilling and balanced professional life. As mindfulness becomes a staple in the corporate world, it paves the way for a new era of business that values mental clarity, emotional intelligence, and the power of presence as key components of success.

Harmonizing the Scales: Mastering Work-Life Balance in Today's Corporate World

In the relentless pursuit of professional success within high-pressure environments, the delicate equilibrium of work-life balance is often disturbed, leading to many stress-related issues and a decline in overall well-being. Maintaining a healthy work-life balance is, therefore not just a desirable skill but a crucial necessity for business professionals in modern times. This article delves into the various strategies and techniques individuals can employ to achieve this balance, ensuring their professional pursuits do not overshadow the essential aspects of personal life and well-being.

The concept of work-life balance is predicated on the understanding that both professional and personal life are integral components of a fulfilling existence. However, this balance is frequently tipped in high-pressure work environments, with work demands encroaching upon personal time and space. The repercussions of this imbalance are far-reaching, impacting not only individual health and happiness but also work efficiency and productivity.

The first step towards restoring this balance is the establishment of clear boundaries. Setting definitive boundaries becomes imperative in an era where technology has blurred the lines between work and home. This involves delineating specific work hours and adhering to them, resisting the urge to constantly check work emails or messages during personal time constantly, and making a conscious effort to physically and mentally disconnect from work once the workday ends. Boundaries are not just a means of separating two aspects of life; they are a statement of prioritization, signifying the value placed on personal time and space.

Equally important in the pursuit of work-life balance is recognising the importance of downtime. Downtime, or time spent away from work-related activities, is essential for mental and emotional rejuvenation. It offers an opportunity to engage in hobbies, spend time with loved ones, or relax and unwind. Downtime should not be viewed as a luxury or an afterthought but as a critical component of a well-rounded life. During these periods of rest and relaxation, individuals often find clarity, creativity, and a renewed sense of purpose, which can subsequently enhance their professional performance.

An integral part of achieving work-life balance is the effective management of time. Time management is not just about organizing work schedules or meeting deadlines; it's about allocating time wisely to ensure that both work and personal life receive adequate attention. This involves prioritizing tasks, setting realistic goals, and being mindful of how time is spent during the workday. Time management also extends to the ability to delegate tasks when necessary. Delegation is often overlooked as a key strategy in maintaining balance, yet it is vital in reducing personal workload and stress. By entrusting responsibilities to others, individuals can free up their time to focus on high-priority tasks and personal well-being.

However, achieving a healthy work-life balance in a high-pressure environment is not solely the individual's responsibility. Employers play a significant role in fostering an environment that supports this balance. This can include implementing flexible working hours, providing resources for stress management, and cultivating a workplace culture that respects personal time and boundaries. Employers who recognize the importance of work-life balance not only contribute to the well-being of their employees but also benefit from increased morale, lower turnover rates, and higher productivity.

Mastering the art of work-life balance in today's high-pressure corporate world is a multifaceted endeavour. It requires a conscious effort to set boundaries, value downtime, manage time effectively, and delegate tasks judiciously. Achieving this balance is not a one-time task but an ongoing process that demands continuous attention and adjustment. By successfully balancing work demands with personal life's needs, individuals can enjoy a more fulfilling, productive, and stress-free existence. In turn, businesses that support and encourage work-life balance are likely to foster a more engaged, motivated, and loyal workforce, ultimately contributing to the success and sustainability of the organization.

Blending Professional Roles with Personal Beliefs

In the corporate corridors where professional achievements often overshadow personal values, nurturing spiritual growth within the workplace emerges as a vital element for creating a more fulfilling and meaningful work environment. This exploration delves into how individuals can intertwine their personal spiritual beliefs with their professional roles, fostering a workplace that resonates with a deeper sense of purpose and fulfilment. It also sheds light on building a spiritually supportive work atmosphere, where diverse beliefs and practices are acknowledged, respected, and celebrated.

The quest for spiritual growth in the workplace is anchored in the belief that our professional and personal lives are not separate entities but intertwined aspects of our overall existence. This belief challenges the conventional view that spirituality is confined to personal spaces and religious contexts, proposing instead that the workplace can be a fertile ground for spiritual exploration and expression.

One of the fundamental steps in cultivating spiritual growth at work is aligning personal values with professional roles. This alignment involves introspection and deeply understanding one's core values and beliefs. It's about asking questions such as, "What values drive me?" "How can these values be reflected in my work?" and "In what ways can my job contribute to my spiritual journey?" By answering these questions, individuals can find ways to infuse their daily tasks with a sense of purpose that aligns with their spiritual beliefs.

For instance, if compassion and empathy are core values for someone, they can find ways to incorporate these into their interactions with colleagues and clients. This might involve being more understanding during negotiations, offering support to team members, or advocating for ethical business practices. Similarly, someone who values creativity and innovation as spiritual expressions can seek roles or projects to explore new ideas and bring fresh perspectives to their work.

Creating a spiritually supportive work environment is another crucial aspect. This type of environment is one where there's an inherent respect for diverse beliefs and practices. It's an atmosphere where employees feel comfortable sharing their spiritual views without fear of judgment or discrimination. Companies can foster such environments by organizing interfaith dialogues, meditation sessions, or workshops on spirituality and work-life balance. These initiatives promote understanding and respect among employees with different beliefs and enrich the workplace culture with diverse perspectives and ideas.

Moreover, employers play a crucial role in cultivating spiritual growth in the workplace. They can do so by encouraging work-life balance, providing opportunities for personal development, and creating policies that respect and accommodate religious and spiritual practices. Employers who recognize the importance of spiritual well-being in their workforce will likely see benefits such as increased employee satisfaction, lower turnover rates, and a more harmonious work environment.

However, cultivating spiritual growth in the workplace is not without its challenges. One of the primary challenges is maintaining a balance between respecting individual spiritual expressions and ensuring that they do not conflict with professional responsibilities or the rights of other employees. This delicate balance requires a deep understanding of and commitment to inclusivity and diversity.

In conclusion, cultivating spiritual growth in the workplace offers a pathway to a more fulfilling and enriching professional life. By aligning personal values with professional roles and creating a spiritually supportive work environment, individuals and organizations can foster a sense of purpose and fulfilment that transcends the mere pursuit of professional achievements. As the corporate world continues to evolve, the integration of spirituality into the workplace stands as a testament to the holistic development of both individuals and organizations, paving the way for a work culture that values not just what we do, but also who we are and what we believe in.

Harnessing Inner Strength in the Corporate Arena

In the labyrinth of the corporate world, where challenges and uncertainties are as certain as the ticking clock, spiritual resilience emerges as an essential tool for navigating these complexities. This article delves into the realm of developing spiritual resilience - a fortitude that empowers professionals to withstand the storms of business life, from the fear of failure to the pressures of competition. It's a journey that transcends the mere acquisition of skills or strategies, delving deeper into how spiritual practices and perspectives offer solace, strength, and guidance in the face of professional adversities.

The concept of spiritual resilience in business is not about religious tenets or rituals but about cultivating an inner stronghold, a sanctuary of peace and strength that can be drawn upon in challenging times. It's about adopting a mindset and practices that foster endurance, positivity, and a sense of hope, even when the business landscape looks daunting.

One of the primary aspects of cultivating this resilience is learning to draw strength from one's spiritual beliefs. Whether it's a belief in a higher power, the interconnectedness of all beings, or the power of positivity, these beliefs can act as an anchor in turbulent times. For instance, believing in a larger purpose or plan can help individuals see beyond the immediate setbacks and view challenges as opportunities for growth and learning.

The power of positive thinking plays a pivotal role in building spiritual resilience. It's about maintaining a mindset that looks for solutions rather than dwelling on problems that see opportunities in obstacles. This positive outlook is not about ignoring the realities of business challenges but approaching them with a mindset open to possibilities and growth. It's about affirming one's abilities and the potential for success, even when circumstances seem dire.

Another crucial element in developing spiritual resilience is maintaining a hopeful outlook. Hope is a powerful force; it propels individuals forward, encourages them to envision a better future, and fuels persistence in adversity. In business, a hopeful outlook can be the difference between giving up and finding a new path to success. It's about believing in one's ability to overcome challenges, adapt, and emerge stronger.

Dealing with failure is an integral part of this journey. Failure, often feared and stigmatized in the corporate world, is, in fact, a vital component of professional growth. Viewing failure through a spiritual lens allows individuals to learn from their mistakes to see failure as a stepping stone to greater wisdom and success. This perspective encourages a more compassionate and forgiving attitude towards oneself and others when mistakes are made, fostering a learning culture rather than blame.

Navigating uncertainty and intense competition also requires spiritual resilience. In an ever-changing business landscape, where nothing is guaranteed, this resilience helps individuals remain centred and focused. It equips them to face competition not with fear, but with a spirit of healthy rivalry and a belief in their unique value and capabilities.

Cultivating spiritual resilience in business is about building an inner sanctuary of strength, positivity, and hope. It's about aligning one's spiritual beliefs with professional endeavours, viewing challenges as opportunities for growth, and maintaining a positive, hopeful outlook. This resilience enhances individual well-being and contributes to a more supportive, compassionate, and enduring business culture. As professionals embrace this journey, they find that they are better equipped to navigate the challenges of their corporate roles and contribute to a more spiritually enriched and resilient business world.

Ch 14. Adapting to Change: Embracing growth and change in business and spirituality

Change is the only constant in the journey of life, both in the realms of business and spirituality. Chapter 14, "Adapting to Change: Embracing Growth and Change in Business and Spirituality," is a deep dive into this inescapable reality, offering insights and strategies to navigate the waters of change with grace and resilience. This chapter explores how the unpredictable tides of the business world, intertwined with the personal evolution of one's spiritual journey, demand a dynamic approach to adaptation and growth.

At the heart of this chapter lies the understanding that change, though often perceived as daunting, is the catalyst for growth and innovation. Change takes many forms in business - from shifts in market dynamics and technological advancements to evolving consumer behaviours and global economic trends. These changes, while challenging, present opportunities for businesses to innovate, grow, and stay competitive. Similarly, in the spiritual journey, change is an invitation to deepen understanding, expand consciousness, and foster personal growth.

The chapter begins by unravelling the nature of change in the business landscape. It offers a perspective that views change not as a hurdle to be overcome but as an integral part of the business lifecycle. This section underscores the importance of recognizing the signs of change and the need for businesses to remain agile and informed. It highlights how being attuned to the nuances of change can empower businesses to make proactive decisions rather than reactive adjustments.

Next, the focus shifts to personal resilience in times of change. Change, especially in a high-stakes business environment, can be a source of significant stress and uncertainty. This section provides strategies and practices to build personal resilience, enabling individuals to maintain equilibrium amidst the flux. It emphasizes the importance of mental and emotional well-being and the role of a supportive network in navigating personal and professional transitions.

This chapter's key component is exploring spiritual approaches to managing change. Here, the discourse delves into how spiritual practices such as meditation, mindfulness, and reflective contemplation can be potent tools in adapting to change. These practices offer a way to maintain inner balance and clarity, providing a stable foundation to embrace external changes.

Innovating and evolving business models in response to change is another crucial topic covered in this chapter. It discusses how businesses can stay relevant and thrive by continually innovating and adapting their strategies to align with new market realities. This section also explores how companies can stay true to their core values and spiritual principles while navigating these changes, ensuring that their evolution is profitable and purposeful.

The chapter concludes with a discussion on cultivating a continuous learning and growth culture. It advocates for creating a workplace environment that values and encourages learning, upskilling, and personal development. This culture enables businesses to adapt effectively to change and fosters a sense of value and investment in employees' professional and spiritual growth.

Essentially, this is a guide for those seeking to gracefully navigate the inevitable changes in their professional and spiritual lives. It provides a roadmap for embracing change not as a force to be feared, but as an opportunity for growth, learning, and evolution. As readers journey through this chapter, they will discover that the art of adapting to change is not merely a skill to be mastered but a dance to be enjoyed, a dance that enriches both their business acumen and spiritual depth.

Decoding the Dynamics of Change in the Business World

In the intricate tapestry of the business world, change is not just an occasional disturbance but a constant, underlying rhythm. Understanding the nature of change within the business context is crucial for any organization seeking to survive and thrive. This article explores the multifaceted nature of business change, examining how it is an inevitable and often beneficial aspect of the commercial landscape, propelled by technological advancements, market trends, and shifts in consumer behavior. It also delves into recognizing the signs of impending change and underscores the importance of agility and informed decision-making in today's fast-paced business environment.

The business landscape is perpetually in motion, influenced by various factors that drive change. Technology is one of the most significant catalysts of change in recent times. Technological advancements have revolutionized the way businesses operate, from automating processes to opening new channels of customer interaction. The digital revolution, characterized by the rise of the internet, social media, and mobile technology, has transformed traditional business models, necessitating an adaptive approach to remain relevant and competitive.

Another driving force behind change in business is market trends. Market dynamics continually evolve, influenced by economic factors, competitive activities, and regulatory changes. Staying attuned to these trends is vital for businesses to anticipate shifts in the market and adapt their strategies accordingly. For instance, the increasing emphasis on sustainability and ethical practices has led many companies to reevaluate their operational practices and align with these emerging market expectations.

Consumer behaviour is also a critical driver of change in the business world. As societal values and lifestyles evolve, so do the preferences and expectations of consumers. Businesses must be adept at understanding these changes in consumer behaviour to tailor their products, services, and marketing strategies effectively. The rise of conscious consumerism, for example, has seen a growing number of consumers prioritize products and services that are environmentally friendly and socially responsible, influencing companies to adapt their offerings to meet these preferences.

Recognizing the signs of impending change is a skill businesses must develop to navigate the unpredictable corporate world. These signs can be subtle, like gradual shifts in customer feedback, or more pronounced, such as a sudden drop in sales or the emergence of a disruptive competitor. Identifying these early indicators of change allows businesses to respond proactively rather than reactively, positioning them to capitalize on opportunities or mitigate potential risks.

Stay informed and agile in this ever-changing landscape cannot be overstated. Agility in business is about the ability to quickly and effectively adapt to change, whether it's altering a marketing strategy, adopting new technologies, or pivoting the entire business model. This agility is underpinned by a culture of continuous learning and innovation, where businesses are perpetually exploring new ideas, experimenting with new approaches, and learning from both successes and failures.

Understanding the nature of business change is fundamental for any organization aiming to succeed in today's dynamic commercial environment. Change, driven by technology, market trends, and consumer behaviour, is a constant feature of the business landscape. Recognizing the signs of this change and maintaining agility are key to ensuring that businesses not only withstand the challenges but also seize the opportunities that change brings. By embracing change as an inherent and beneficial aspect of business, organizations can foster a culture of adaptability, innovation, and sustained growth.

In this context, embracing change requires more than just tactical adjustments; it demands a strategic rethinking of business models and practices. Companies must cultivate a forward-thinking mindset that views change not as a threat but as an opportunity for growth and innovation. This mindset is crucial for fostering a culture that is resilient, adaptive, and prepared for the future.

One of the critical strategies in navigating business change is effective communication. Clear and transparent communication within the organization is vital during times of change. It helps manage expectations, reduce uncertainties, and ensure that all organisation members are aligned with the new direction or strategy. Effective communication also involves listening to employee, customer, and stakeholder feedback, which can provide valuable insights and help fine-tune the approach to change.

Another important aspect is risk management. Change often brings risks, and managing these risks proactively is essential. This involves identifying potential risks associated with change, assessing their impact, and developing mitigation strategies. Risk management prepares the organization for potential setbacks and ensures that the process of adapting to change is smooth and sustainable.

Investing in technology and innovation is also crucial in adapting to change. Technology can be a powerful enabler of change, helping businesses to streamline operations, enhance customer experiences, and create new value propositions. Staying abreast of technological advancements and integrating them into business operations can provide a significant competitive edge.

Leadership plays a pivotal role in steering an organization through change. Influential leaders are those who can inspire and motivate their teams, even in the face of uncertainty and challenges. They are visionaries who can articulate a clear vision of the future and rally their teams around it. Leadership during times of change involves being decisive yet empathetic, confident yet open to new ideas, and steadfast yet flexible.

Finally, embracing change in business is about fostering a culture of continuous learning and development. A learning culture encourages employees to develop new skills, stay curious, and be open to new ways of thinking. This culture is vital for an organization's ability to adapt to change, ensuring that the workforce is equipped to handle new challenges and seize new opportunities.

In essence, adapting to change in the business world is a multifaceted process that requires strategic thinking, effective communication, risk management, technological integration, strong leadership, and a culture of continuous learning. By embracing these elements, businesses can not only navigate the complexities of change but also emerge stronger and more resilient. The ability to adapt to change is not just a survival skill in the corporate world; it is a fundamental driver of growth, innovation, and long-term success.

Staying Afloat: Cultivating Personal Resilience Amidst Professional Upheaval

In the whirlwind of professional life, change is inevitable. It sweeps through the workplace in various forms—restructuring, shifting market dynamics, or new leadership directions. Such periods of transition are not just organizational challenges but deeply personal ones, requiring individuals to summon their inner strength and adaptability. This exploration into building personal resilience offers insights into maintaining mental and emotional well-being during these turbulent times, highlighting effective stress management techniques and the critical role of a supportive network.

Resilience, in essence, is the ability to bounce back from adversity, to face challenges head-on and emerge stronger. While partly innate, it's a quality that can be nurtured and developed with intentional practices and strategies. The journey towards cultivating personal resilience begins with self-awareness—recognizing one's emotional responses to change and understanding that feeling disoriented or stressed is a natural reaction. Acknowledging these feelings is the first step in managing them effectively.

One of the foundational elements of resilience is stress management. In times of change, stress levels can skyrocket, impairing one's ability to think clearly and make reasoned decisions. Techniques such as mindfulness meditation, deep breathing exercises, and regular physical activity can mitigate stress. Mindfulness meditation, for instance, helps anchor one's attention in the present moment, creating a space of calm amidst the storm of change. Deep breathing exercises can quickly lower stress levels, while physical activity releases endorphins, boosting mood and energy levels.

Equally important to personal resilience is the cultivation of a positive mindset. This doesn't mean ignoring the realities of challenging situations but rather focusing on what can be controlled and looking for opportunities for growth within adversity. A positive mindset is characterized by optimism, the practice of gratitude, and the willingness to learn from every situation. Optimism doesn't deny the difficulty but chooses to see beyond it, believing in one's capacity to navigate through. Practising gratitude shifts focus from what's lacking to what's present, while a learning mindset turns obstacles into lessons, fostering personal and professional growth.

However, resilience isn't solely an internal endeavor; the role of a supportive network is indispensable. During times of significant change, having a network of colleagues, mentors, friends, or family to lean on can make a profound difference. These relationships provide emotional support, practical advice, and a sense of belonging, buffering against the isolating effects of stress and uncertainty. A supportive network also offers diverse perspectives, helping to see situations in a new light and uncovering solutions that might not have been apparent.

Moreover, resilience involves proactive self-care. In the pursuit of adapting to workplace changes, it's crucial not to neglect one's physical and emotional well-being. This means setting aside time for activities that rejuvenate and fulfill, whether it's pursuing a hobby, spending time with loved ones, or simply resting. Self-care is a critical component of resilience, ensuring individuals have the energy and emotional capacity to face the challenges ahead.

Cultivating personal resilience in times of change is a multifaceted process that involves managing stress, fostering a positive mindset, drawing on the strength of a supportive network, and engaging in proactive self-care. It's about navigating the ebb and flow of professional life with grace, learning from each experience, and emerging not just intact but invigorated. As individuals develop their capacity for resilience, they enhance their ability to adapt to change and contribute to a more resilient workplace culture, where challenges are met with courage, creativity, and a collective strength.

Anchoring the Soul: Spiritual Wisdom for Navigating Change

In the ceaseless tide of life's changes, particularly within the high-stakes environment of the business world, individuals often seek solid ground. Amidst the flux of market dynamics, organizational shifts, and the personal upheaval these can cause, spiritual practices offer a refuge, a means to anchor the soul in something deeper and more enduring. This article explores how spiritual approaches, such as meditation, mindfulness, and reflective contemplation, serve as powerful tools for managing and adapting to change, ensuring individuals maintain inner balance and clarity.

Change, by its very nature, tends to unsettle the status quo, often leaving a trail of stress and anxiety in its wake. With its inherent unpredictability, the business world serves as a prime catalyst for such change, challenging individuals to continuously adapt. Yet, it is within this environment that spiritual practices can shine, offering pathways to not only survive but thrive through change.

Meditation stands out as a cornerstone spiritual practice for managing change. Meditation fosters a deep sense of calm and centeredness by encouraging individuals to sit quietly with their thoughts, without judgment or immediate reaction. This practice allows individuals to detach from the whirlwind of external circumstances and connect with a place of inner stillness. Over time, regular meditation cultivates a mental resilience that can weather the storms of change, enabling a response to challenges from a place of wisdom rather than knee-jerk reactivity.

Mindfulness, closely related to meditation, emphasizes the importance of being fully present in the moment. In the context of navigating change, mindfulness transforms everyday activities into exercises in awareness, teaching individuals to notice their reactions to change without becoming overwhelmed by them. This heightened state of awareness can lead to clearer thinking and better decision-making, as individuals learn to observe the ebb and flow of their emotions without being capsized by them.

Reflective contemplation, another spiritual tool, encourages a deeper exploration of one's responses to change. By reflecting on past experiences of change, individuals can gain insights into their patterns of behaviour and thought, learning from them to better navigate future changes. Reflective contemplation can also involve considering the broader implications of change, both personally and professionally, helping to align actions with deeper values and purposes.

The integration of these spiritual practices into daily life demands intention and discipline but offers profound rewards. Individuals who engage in these practices often report increased emotional stability, improved mental clarity, and a stronger sense of purpose. Moreover, these practices foster a sense of connection to something greater than oneself, whether that is a community, the natural world, or a higher power. This sense of connection can be incredibly grounding in times of change, providing a broader perspective and a reminder of the interconnectedness of all things.

In conclusion, as the business world continues to evolve at an ever-accelerating pace, the need for effective tools to manage change becomes increasingly apparent. Spiritual practices like meditation, mindfulness, and reflective contemplation offer valuable resources for maintaining inner balance and clarity amidst external changes. By anchoring the soul in these practices, individuals can navigate the waters of change with grace, resilience, and a deep sense of peace.

Navigating the Winds of Change: The Art of Innovating and Evolving Business Models

In the ever-evolving landscape of the business world, adaptability is the key to survival and success. As markets shift, consumer preferences change, and new technologies emerge, businesses must be ready to pivot and transform their strategies to stay relevant and competitive. This article explores the practical aspects of adapting business models in response to change, emphasizing the importance of innovation, flexibility, and alignment with core values and spiritual principles.

Embracing Change as a Constant: Change is a constant companion in the fast-paced global marketplace. Businesses that thrive understand that they must be proactive in anticipating and responding to shifts in their industry, rather than reacting when it's too late. This proactive approach begins with a willingness to embrace change as a fundamental part of the business journey. By recognizing that stagnation is the enemy of progress, companies can lay the foundation for a resilient and adaptable business model.

The Power of Innovation: Innovation is the lifeblood of successful business models. The engine drives growth and allows businesses to stay ahead of the curve. Innovation can take many forms, from developing new products and services to optimising internal processes. By fostering a culture of innovation within the organization, businesses can tap into the creative potential of their employees and continuously explore new avenues for growth.

The Art of Pivoting: Pivoting is a strategic maneuver that can save a business from obsolescence. It involves a deliberate shift in the core strategy or direction of the company in response to changing market dynamics. Pivoting requires a deep understanding of market trends, customer feedback, and the courage to make bold decisions. Successful pivots often involve adapting to new technologies, entering new markets, or even redefining the company's mission and values.

Evolving While Staying True: Amidst all the changes and innovations, businesses need to maintain a strong sense of identity and purpose. Core values and spiritual principles serve as the compass that guides decision-making, ensuring that every evolution aligns with the company's mission and ethics. It's not about abandoning one's principles to pursue profits but finding creative ways to harmonize growth with the values that define the organization's essence.

Navigating New Market Realities: The business world is marked by constant disruption, and staying ahead of the curve means understanding and adapting to new market realities. This requires a keen sense of market analysis, the ability to spot emerging trends, and the agility to adjust strategies accordingly. Businesses that can pivot swiftly to capitalize on opportunities or mitigate threats are more likely to thrive in a rapidly changing landscape.

The Role of Leadership: Effective leadership plays a pivotal role in innovating and evolving business models. Leaders must inspire and empower their teams to embrace change and foster a culture of innovation. They should also lead by example, demonstrating a willingness to adapt and learn. Strong leadership guides the organization through the challenging transitions that accompany any strategic shift.

Learning from Failure: Innovation and evolution often come with risks, and not every change will yield immediate success. Businesses should view failure as a valuable learning opportunity rather than a setback. Each failure provides insights that can inform future strategies and lead to more robust, resilient business models. Adapting and persevering in the face of setbacks is a hallmark of successful organizations.

Sustainability and Ethical Considerations: As businesses innovate and evolve, it's vital to consider their impact on society and the environment. Sustainable and ethical practices are becoming increasingly important to consumers and stakeholders alike. Incorporating sustainability into a business model's core can enhance its reputation and contribute to long-term viability in a world where environmental and social concerns are paramount.

Innovation and the ability to evolve are not just buzzwords in the business world but essential survival skills. Businesses that recognize the need for continuous adaptation and align their strategies with their core values and spiritual principles are better equipped to navigate the ever-changing landscape. In a world where change is the only constant, the journey towards a successful business model is an ongoing process of innovation, flexibility, and staying true to one's guiding principles.

Nurturing Growth: Building a Workplace Culture of Continuous Learning and Development

In today's dynamic business environment, one of the most significant assets a company can possess is a culture that values continuous learning and growth. This culture empowers employees to adapt to change and fosters an environment where personal and professional development are at the forefront. This article delves into the importance of cultivating a workplace culture that embraces learning and growth as fundamental values, exploring how it can drive business success and create a sense of purpose and fulfilment for employees.

The Essence of a Learning Culture: A learning culture is more than just offering training programs or workshops. It's about creating an environment where curiosity is encouraged, mistakes are seen as learning opportunities, and employees are continually inspired to develop their skills and knowledge. A workplace that values learning adapts to change more effectively and attracts and retains top talent seeking personal and professional growth.

Continuous Learning: A Key to Adaptation: In an ever-evolving business landscape, organizations that fail to adapt risk becoming obsolete. Constant learning is the antidote to stagnation, as it equips employees with the tools they need to stay relevant. When employees are encouraged to update their skills and regularly stay informed about industry trends, the company becomes better equipped to respond to market changes and emerging opportunities.

Investing in Upskilling: Investing in upskilling is a critical aspect of fostering a culture of continuous learning. This involves providing employees with opportunities to acquire or enhance new skills. Upskilling benefits the individual and bolsters the organization's capabilities, leading to increased efficiency and innovation. Companies prioritising upskilling are more likely to be on the cutting edge of their industry.

The Link Between Growth and Engagement: Employees who perceive that their organization values their growth are more engaged and committed. A continuous learning and development culture demonstrates that the company cares about its employees' well-being and prospects. This, in turn, leads to higher job satisfaction, improved performance, and reduced turnover rates.

Personal Development as a Cornerstone: Embracing personal development as a core value goes beyond professional growth. It recognizes employees as multidimensional individuals with personal aspirations, values, and spiritual principles. Encouraging personal development aligns with the idea that a fulfilling life extends beyond the workplace, and a supportive employer can be instrumental in helping employees achieve their personal goals.

Empowering Employees to Take Ownership: In a culture of continuous learning and growth, employees are not passive recipients of knowledge but active participants in their own development. Empowering employees to take ownership of their learning journey by setting goals, seeking out resources, and embracing challenges can lead to more motivated and self-reliant individuals who contribute positively to the organization.

Leadership's Role in Fostering Growth: Leaders play a pivotal role in shaping an organisation's culture. Their actions and behaviors set the tone for what is valued within the company. Effective leaders actively support and model continuous learning and development, making it clear that growth is a shared commitment. They also provide mentorship and coaching to nurture the skills and potential of their team members.

Measuring and Recognizing Progress: To sustain a continuous learning and growth culture, measuring and recognising progress is essential. This can be done through regular feedback, performance evaluations, and acknowledging accomplishments. Celebrating both individual and collective achievements reinforces the culture and encourages employees to continue their development journey.

Building a workplace culture that embraces continuous learning and development is not just a business strategy; it's a commitment to the well-being and growth of both the organization and its employees. Such a culture fosters adaptability, engagement, and a sense of purpose, creating a positive cycle of success. By investing in the continuous learning and growth of its workforce, a company thrives in the present. It secures a brighter future for itself and its employees, aligning with its core values and spiritual principles.

Ch 15. Legacy and Impact: Envisioning the long-term spiritual impact of your entrepreneurial journey

In entrepreneurship, financial gains, market share, and profitability often measure success. However, a deeper dimension to the entrepreneurial journey transcends the balance sheets and spreadsheets. This dimension is all about legacy and impact—the lasting spiritual imprint your business leaves on the world. In this article, we will explore the concept of legacy and how it relates to your entrepreneurial journey. We'll encourage you, the reader, to reflect on what you want to leave behind and how you want to be remembered. Moreover, we will discuss the profound connection between your values, spiritual beliefs, and the legacy you wish to create through your business.

Legacy is not just about material wealth or the tangible assets you accumulate throughout your entrepreneurial career. It encompasses your intangible, enduring impact on people, communities, and the world. Your legacy is the essence of your existence long after you've moved on. It's the mark you leave on the hearts and minds of those you've touched.

Your entrepreneurial journey is a unique path that offers an incredible opportunity to shape your legacy. Every decision you make, every action you take, and every relationship you nurture contributes to the story of your business and, by extension, your personal legacy. But how can you ensure that your legacy is spiritually aligned with your beliefs and values?

To begin envisioning the long-term spiritual impact of your entrepreneurial journey, take some time for introspection. Ask yourself these questions:

> **What do I want to leave behind?** Consider the qualities, principles, and values you wish to imprint on your business, employees, and customers. Think about the positive change you want to bring to the world through your work.

How do I want to be remembered? Reflect on the lasting impressions you want to make on people's lives. Consider the kind of stories you want them to tell about you and your business, and how those stories align with your spiritual beliefs.

What are my core values and spiritual beliefs? Take an inventory of your personal values and spiritual convictions. How can these beliefs be integrated into your entrepreneurial journey and serve as the foundation for the legacy you want to create?

Aligning Values and Legacy

Your values and spiritual beliefs should serve as guiding stars on your entrepreneurial journey. They provide the compass by which you navigate challenges, make decisions, and set goals. When you align your business practices with your deeply held values, you create a powerful synergy that fosters a spiritually aligned legacy.

Consider the following steps:

Integrate Values into Your Business: Embed your core values into your company's mission statement, culture, and practices. Ensure that every aspect of your business reflects these principles.

Lead by Example: As an entrepreneur, you are the driving force behind your business. Demonstrate your commitment to your values and beliefs through your actions, decisions, and interactions with others.

Inspire Others: Encourage your employees, partners, and stakeholders to share in your spiritual vision. When your team is aligned with your values, they become ambassadors of your legacy.

Your entrepreneurial journey is not just a quest for profit; it's a sacred opportunity to leave a lasting, spiritually aligned legacy. By exploring the concept of legacy, reflecting on what you want to leave behind, and connecting your personal values and spiritual beliefs to your business, you can create a profound and positive impact on the world. Remember that the legacy you envision today has the potential to inspire generations to come, making your entrepreneurial journey a meaningful and spiritually fulfilling endeavour.

Integrating spiritual insights into business success

As we arrive at the final chapter of "Entrepreneurial Enlightenment: Secrets to Building a Spiritually-Aligned Business," it's time to reflect on the transformative journey we've embarked upon together. Throughout this book, we've explored the profound connection between entrepreneurship and spirituality, unlocking the secrets to building a business that not only thrives in the material sense but also resonates deeply with our innermost values and beliefs. As we conclude this enlightening journey, let's revisit some key takeaways and part with a renewed sense of purpose and vision.

We began our journey by acknowledging the intersection of spirituality and entrepreneurship. In a world often driven by profit margins and market competition, we discovered a higher purpose to our entrepreneurial endeavours—one that goes beyond financial success. Its purpose involves personal growth, the betterment of society, and the alignment of our business aspirations with our spiritual values.

Throughout the book, we've delved into various aspects of building a spiritually-aligned business. We've learned that it starts with self-awareness, as understanding our own values, beliefs, and purpose lays the foundation for an enlightened entrepreneurial journey. We've explored the importance of ethical decision-making, fostering a conscious company culture, and nurturing relationships based on trust and respect.

One recurring theme in our exploration is the power of purpose-driven entrepreneurship. We've uncovered that when we infuse our businesses with a clear sense of purpose that reflects our spiritual values, we attract like-minded customers and partners and find a deeper fulfilment in our work. Purpose becomes the guiding star that steers us through challenges and fuels our resilience.

Another central theme of our journey has been creating a positive impact. We've seen that a spiritually-aligned business goes beyond profit and measures success by the positive change it brings to individuals, communities, and the world. From ethical sourcing to sustainable practices and community engagement, we've explored the myriad ways businesses can become a force for good.

In our chapter on "Legacy and Impact," we delved into the notion that our entrepreneurial journey is a vehicle for leaving a lasting legacy. This legacy embodies our spiritual beliefs and values. We discussed how your legacy is not just about material wealth but the imprint you leave on the hearts and minds of others. By aligning your business with your spiritual values, you have the potential to inspire generations to come.

As we conclude our journey towards entrepreneurial enlightenment, remember it's an ongoing process. Your business is not static; it evolves, just as you do. Embrace change and adapt as your understanding of your values and purpose deepens. Stay true to the principles that resonate with you, and continue to seek enlightenment through your entrepreneurial path.

Your commitment to building a spiritually-aligned business will set you apart in this ever-evolving business world, where challenges and opportunities abound. It will empower you to navigate the complexities of entrepreneurship with grace, wisdom, and compassion.

In closing, let's carry forward the wisdom gained from this journey and let it guide our entrepreneurial endeavours. May your business be not just a source of profit but a beacon of spiritual alignment and positive impact. Together, as enlightened entrepreneurs, we have the potential to reshape the world—one spiritually-aligned business at a time. Thank you for joining us on this transformative voyage towards Entrepreneurial Enlightenment.

About the Author

Alex Wealthfield, unveils a fresh perspective on business success. Rooted in his own journey, Alex's work explores the fusion of personal values and spiritual beliefs with the entrepreneurial world. He offers practical insights, exercises, and reflections, guiding readers to create businesses that enrich lives and leave a lasting impact. Alex Wealthfield is your ally in embracing a higher purpose in entrepreneurship, redefining success, and achieving fulfilment in the business world.

9 789358 815368